The White Monk

The White Monk

An Essay on Dostoevsky and Melville

by

F. D. Reeve

VANDERBILT UNIVERSITY PRESS
Nashville, Tennessee
1989

Acknowledgments

My thanks to the American Council of Learned Societies, which awarded a grant for research; to those anonymous readers who directed the manuscript toward its final shape; to Robert Belknap, critic and professor, who saw some early chapters and made helpful suggestions; to Sonia Ketchian, scholar, and the Russian Research Center at Harvard for arranging a lively seminar around the argument of the middle chapters; to the late Theodore Morrison, poet and novelist, director of Breadloaf, who read it with the wisdom of years of writing; and to John Thurner, novelist, who responded to the first draft with enthusiasm and many paragraphs of careful, pointed commentary.

Transliteration / Translation

In the text, for readability I have followed a conventional transliteration of Russian, which gives *Dostoevsky* and *Chekhov,* for example. In the notes and bibliography, I have used the literal scheme, in which each Cyrillic letter is represented by a Latin, giving *Dostoevskij* and *Čexov.*

Uncredited translations are mine.

Published in 1989 by Vanderbilt University Press
Printed in the United States of America

Library of Congress Cataloging-in-Publication Data

Reeve, F. D. (Franklin D.), 1928-
The white monk : an essay on Dostoevsky & Melville / F.D. Reeve.
p. cm.
Bibliography: p.
Includes index.
ISBN 0-8265-1234-8 : $17.95 (est.)
1. Dostoyevsky, Fyodor, 1821-1881—Criticism and interpretation.
2. Melville, Herman, 1819-1891—Criticism and interpretation.
3. Literature, Comparative—Russian and American. 4. Literature, Comparative—American and Russian. I. Title.
PG3328.R35 1989 89-35562
813'.3—dc20 CIP

Contents

1

Inner Self / Outer World

> The world is as young to-day as when it was created; and this Vermont morning dew is as wet to my feet as Eden's dew to Adam's. . . . All that has been said, but multiplies the avenues to what remains to be said.
>
> —*Melville*

USUALLY CALLED THE AGE OF ENLIGHTENment or the Age of Reason, the eighteenth century seems distinguished by a pervasive intellectual and moral order. Its social harmonies appear as fixed and natural as the stars. From Pope and Johnson to Washington and Jefferson, we think of men bound by faith in fair and rational nature who "hold these truths to be self-evident, that all men are created equal, that they are endowed by their Creator with certain unalienable Rights, that among these are Life, Liberty, and the pursuit of Happiness."

Prudence and experience were the instruments for measuring consent and achieving future security. The French Revolution and the American War of Independence—but not the unsuccessful Pugachëv Rebellion—were extreme and divers forms of the assertion of the "Rights of Man" by which the middle class, as it moved from economic to political power, extended to other classes and peoples without distinction the rights it claimed for itself. "The time will come," Condorcet said, "when the sun will shine only on free men, recognizing no other master than reason; when tyrants and slaves, priests and their stupid or hypocritical tools will exist only in history and on the stage."[1] Place would be no restriction, and cultural prejudice would be overcome. "All men are naturally in . . . a state of perfect freedom to order their actions and dispose of their possessions and persons as they think fit," Locke declared. "Men living together according to reason, without a common superior on earth with authority to judge between them, is properly the state of nature." In a previous essay he had announced that "the sum of all we drive at is that every man may enjoy the same rights that are granted to others."[2]

In Europe and America, the philosophy of materialism and the development of scientific equipment for more nearly accurately measuring the universe did not violate prevailing Christian norms. On the contrary, Christian idealism encouraged humanitarianism, utopism, geographic exploration, and the idea of progress. Intellectuals believed in the perfectibility of man: Because the natural world was rational, man could conquer it and determine his own future by the mechanical means of Newtonian science and the new values of the French encyclopedists.

To every problem the eighteenth-century man of culture assumed there was a correct answer. There was one order of nature and one human hierarchy; so, there was one proper way to write an ode, one proper way to live. Disputes arose not over goals but over qualities of performance:

> Teach him to scorn with frigid art
> Feebly to touch th' unraptured heart!
> Like lightning, let his mighty verse
> The bosom's inmost foldings pierce;
> With native beauties win applause,
> Beyond cold critics' studied laws:
> O let each Muse's fame increase,
> O bid Britannia rival Greece![3]

Built of borrowed materials, the eighteenth-century house of culture seemed to enclose permanence against the raggle-taggle of daily life. Not only was there but one style in music, sculpture, and architecture, but also the posed "conversation piece," a portrait of a gentle family in elegant clothes on a greensward against a backdrop of open fields and country villas, seemed literally to insist that economic and social refinement faithfully measured the things of this world.

Romanticism protested the partiality of this view. It honored the autonomy of individuality and the power of emotion as sources of truth. The eighteenth-century intellectual scheme, the romantics said, was an improperly aristocratic, false humanism. Because it could neither justify the deprivations that most men humbly suffered nor tolerate the willful, imaginative deviations of those who, like Sterne, irreverently, ironically declared that they designed their fictions to "teach us to love the world and our fellow creatures better than we do,"[4] it had to be overthrown. The source of evil, Rousseau wrote in *Émile,* was not the discrepancy between man's accomplishment and his goals, between the *is* and the *ought to be,* but human institutions themselves. "The constitution of a man is the work of nature," he wrote in *The Social Contract*; "that of the state is the work of artifice. . . . When we see among the happiest people in the world bands of peasants regulating the affairs of state under an oak tree, and always acting wisely, can we help feeling a certain contempt for the refinements of other nations, which employ so much skill and mystery to make themselves at once illustrious and wretched?"[5]

In both America and Russia, the period 1775–1825 marked vigorous colonial expansion. Under Catherine the Great (1762–96) Russia swelled both east and west, but most important was the conquest of the Black Sea steppes stretching from the Danube to the Caucasus and making Russia one of the granaries of Europe. During Catherine's reign, population nearly doubled from twenty million to thirty-six million, of which almost 95 percent was rural and 3 percent urban; the nobility and landed gentry comprised slightly over 2 percent. Important factories and mills, most but not all state-owned, doubled; exports increased 4.5 times and imports, 5 times. At the end of the American Revolution, the thirteen states had about three million people; within twenty years, through Napoleon's sale of the Louisiana Territory, their area more than doubled, and in another ten, their population had done the same. Western expansion by conquest and by settlement and industrial development, including technological innovation, paralleled each other; as the country grew, so did its total wealth, which from 1787 to 1860 quadrupled. Along with territorial expansion and economic growth came cultural development—newspapers, music societies and operas, literature, painting and sculpture and museums, medical research and scientific inquiry—beginning in both countries in the second half of the eighteenth century and achieving international stature in the nineteenth.

Napoleon's campaigns confirmed the nationalistic realignment of Europe and the romantic democratization of the baroque kingdoms. In the course of the nineteenth century, political reform led to even greater violence and to consolidation of power in central governments, each with a civil service. Lofty old claims of liberty, fraternity, and equality became demagogic jargon. In *Democracy in America*, Tocqueville admired the New World's energy but warned against the tyranny of the majority.

The elimination of slavery did not stop war, disease, and natural catastrophe from restricting population growth to immigration and conquest and from further enriching the rich and impoverishing the poor. Attempts at rationalizing the social order, like Montesquieu's *Laws* in the eighteenth century or the populist movements in the nineteenth, though intended for everyone, in fact applied only to the literate and the propertied. As the court had long been the keeper of the King's English, so the public was thought too common to respond intelligently to an imaginative world. Underneath Joshua Reynolds's conventional objection to cliché and triteness is his conviction that the artist's vocabulary and attitude must be elitist: "Whatever is expressed in common words, colloquial language, is never, nor can be, forcibly expressed to the imagination."[6] A *New Yorker* cartoon of a Bohemian painter declaring apocalyptically, "I paint what I *don't* see," humorously emphasizes the discrepancy between two common assumptions about the artist as a man apart: Self-indulgently and abnormally isolated, the artist slaps fantastic nonsense onto canvas; rejecting the external, bourgeois city of the Philistines, the artist exploits inner turmoil to express the truth of the image. The eighteenth-century ideal was rather different, whether represented by Pope's stylistic exaggeration in satire to express a new, reformist thought based on the singularity of excellence, as in *The Dunciad:*

> In clouded majesty here dulness shone;
> Four guardian virtues, round, support her throne:
> [. . . fortitude . . . temperance . . . prudence . . .]
> Poetic justice, with her lifted scale,
> Where, in nice balance, truth with gold she weighs,
> And solid pudding against empty praise.
> Here she beholds the chaos dark and deep,

> Where nameless somethings in their causes sleep,
> 'Till genial Jacob, or a warm third day,
> Call forth each mass, a poem, or a play:
> How hints, like spawn, scarce quick in embryo lie,
> How new-born nonsense first is taught to cry,
> Maggots half-formed in rhyme exactly meet,
> And learn to crawl upon poetic feet.
> . . . .
> How tragedy and comedy embrace;
> How farce and epic get a jumbled race;
> How Time himself stands still at her command,
> Realms shift their place, and ocean turns to land.[7]

—or stated forthrightly, as in his brief essay in the *Guardian* of September 29, 1713: "I believe it is no wrong observation, that persons of genius, and those who are most capable of art, are always most fond of Nature; as such are chiefly sensible that all art consists in the imitation and study of Nature. On the contrary, people of the common level of understanding . . . constantly think that finest which is least natural." Both Dostoevsky and Melville employed Pope's, Swift's, and Addison's satiric use of the aberrant or bizarre contrasted to a Latinate style as the source of much of their humor, but by their time the idea of nature was entirely different.

What Pope thought natural was circumscribed by Alkinoös's four-acre garden in Book 7 of *The Odyssey* "with trees in bloom or weighted down for picking."[8] The first romantics changed that concept and man's relation to it. No longer a gentleman-observer, the poet seemed to Wordsworth a subtler, more sensitive, more organized shepherd, a man set deeply in nature by need and by faculty. He derived his authority autochthonously, from his necessary participation in the dynamics of the enveloping natural world. He was a sort of supershepherd who, as a man of emotion, could see, think, and feel more than others. Precisely at the time industrialization began to transform nature and to harness its potential energies for human purposes, comfort, and profit, the romantics celebrated the joy of a natural life. The shepherd, who lived in harmony with the fields and streams without changing them, who self-reliantly endured the seasons' change, seemed a giant, and indeed the poet himself, no longer a representative among men but self-consciously an embodiment of Man, dated his birth from the birth of Nature in him:

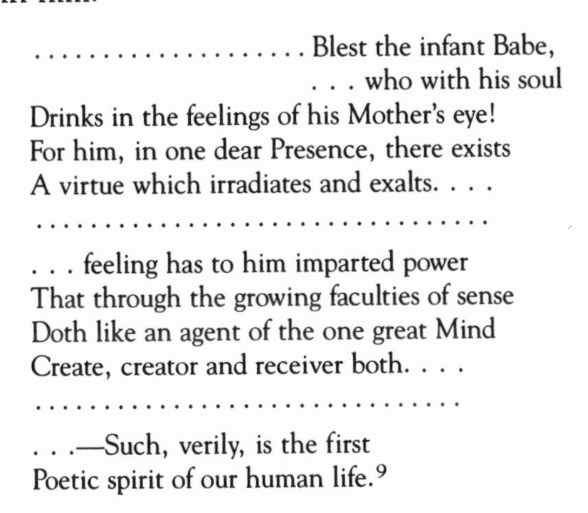

. . . . Blest the infant Babe,
. . . who with his soul
Drinks in the feelings of his Mother's eye!
For him, in one dear Presence, there exists
A virtue which irradiates and exalts. . . .
. . . .

. . . feeling has to him imparted power
That through the growing faculties of sense
Doth like an agent of the one great Mind
Create, creator and receiver both. . . .
. . . .

. . .—Such, verily, is the first
Poetic spirit of our human life.[9]

For Baudelaire a half-century later, tempted and tormented by madness (mon âme est félée), who saw the exterior world only through imagination as through a window frame, the teeming city was dazzling and diabolic: "Voici le soir charmant, ami du criminel."[10] For Wordsworth, the modern city was a "monstrous ant-hill on the plain / Of a too busy world!"[11] His modernism lay in admiration for the principles expressed by the French Revolution, some of which he witnessed in Paris in 1790–92, and in his rejection of commercial, classical, and clerical orthodoxy. Life was joy; experience was mystical; the self housed its own existence and its own transcendence:

> Enough of humble arguments; recall,
> My Song! those high emotions which thy voice
> Has heretofore made known; that bursting forth
> Of sympathy, inspiring and inspired,
> When everywhere a vital pulse was felt,
> And all the several frames of things, like stars,
> Through every magnitude distinguishable,
> Shone mutually indebted, or half lost
> Each in the other's blaze, a galaxy
> Of life and glory. In the midst stood Man,
> Outwardly, inwardly contemplated,
> As, of all visible natures, crown, though born
> Of dust, and kindred to the worm; a Being,
> Both in perception and discernment, first
> In every capability of rapture,
> Through the divine effect of power and love;
> As, more than anything we know, instinct
> With godhead, and, by reason and by will,
> Acknowledging dependency sublime.[12]

Dürer's self-portrait in a veronica, his representation of himself as a sign-carrying marcher in *Martyrdom of the Ten Thousand,* and Dante's self-appointed walk through the middle of *The Divine Comedy* were extraordinary examples of an artist's objectifying his subjectivity and simultaneously romantically heightening the suffering, or pity, felt by acting a central role. Both artists assumed the existence of a boundless Heaven and an absolute moral hierarchy. Wordsworth does not, and so his artist finds the world as much inside himself as outside:

> The Poet is chiefly distinguished from other men by a greater promptness to think and feel without immediate external excitement, and a greater power in expressing such thoughts and feelings as are produced in him in

> that manner . . . [connected to all] the appearances of the visible universe. . . . The Poet thinks and feels in the spirit of human passions. . . . Poetry is the spontaneous overflow of powerful feelings: it takes its origin from emotion recollected in tranquillity; the emotion is contemplated till, by a species of re-action, the tranquillity gradually disappears, and an emotion . . . does itself actually exist in the mind. . . . In describing any passions whatsoever, which are voluntarily described, the mind will, upon the whole, be in a state of enjoyment.[13]

The language of poets, he says, comes from the language of men.

We are now differently democratic, and our idea of grammar has much changed since 1800. Our "ordinary language of literature" embraces a colloquial style more confidently than an aristocratic. We do not immure artistic sensibility even in the woods. In fact, because we assume nature to be limited and public life to be false, if not corrupt, we crave the private, or "true," story, which we equate with artistic expression. The whole job of making sense of human lives in what seems a randomly arranged universe has been dumped on the artist:

> So that's life, then: things as they are?
> It picks its way on the blue guitar.
>
> A million people on one string?
> And all their manner in the thing,
>
> And all their manner, right and wrong,
> And all their manner, weak and strong?
>
> The feelings crazily, craftily call,
> Like a buzzing of flies in autumn air,
>
> And that's life, then: things as they are,
> This buzzing of the blue guitar.[14]

Do the "paradigms" of our tradition encompass the dilemmas of our experience? The world changes. Even if our fathers taught us what they knew, what we have discovered and what we need to know, different between themselves, differ from what they knew—as what they knew differed from what our grandfathers knew. Dostoevsky and Melville were not faced with knowledge of DNA molecular "stickiness" making genetic recombination possible in uncontrollable ways, but they were faced with trains, steamships, and radical social change caused by technological innovation and industrial development. They rebelled against the absurdities of fads and the inconsistencies between ethical standards and social practices. They were not muckrakers exposing practical corruption but moralists pointing out the irresoluble contradictions of a modern life ill-adapted to traditional values. Even as they believed in and supported those values, they understood that modern life made such values inadequate. For example, Thoreau closes *Walden*, that compendium of eighteenth-century ideals of moral absolutism and natural liberty, with a reference to the well-known New England story of the beautiful bug that emerged after sixty years from an applewood table, citing it as an example of man's resurrection from the "dead dry life of society." In his sketch "The Apple-Tree Table," Melville's theme is that sensation, reason, and intuition are all "inadequate for explaining or solving the mystery, which remains after all is said and done still a mystery."[15]

Quaint as the idea of an underlying rational order may seem—science does not affirm it, and nothing in our contemporary societal lives is a model—the idea of progress is incredible, too. Marxist though he was, Antonio Gramsci believed that capitalist economic control did not fully explain social injustice. The crucial factor, he made clear, was not the material hegemony but the spiritual hegemony of the oppressors.[16] The economic system then ran like a lottery, rewarding the few at the expense of the many and holding out illusory hope to all. The prevailing superstructure was an insidious confusion of profit, technology, legerdemain, and art, a "civilized" world of injustice in which armed white men argued about who owned a black man, the world Huck Finn said he did not want to go back to because he had been there before.

It is still true that whoever owns the means of production controls the means of communication. The following appeared as a public advertisement: "The Bell System American Orchestras on Tour Program is taking 30 major symphony orchestras to over 240 cities across the United States. It's our way of helping orchestras reach places and people they might not have reached before—not merely an extension of our business, but a part of it."[17] The illusion that tolerates such hegemony is necessary because men cannot live with the truth. They live with their feelings and with either the neurotic or the creative distortions that follow from them.[18] In that sense, the romanticism of the nineteenth century was not a rebellion against the rationalism of the eighteenth but a continued, sophisticated effort to eliminate arbitrary discrepancies and partial beliefs. When a "committed" artist such as Melville stepped aside from life, he meant not to hypostatize it but to review it:

> With wrecks in a garret I'm stranded,
> Where, no longer returning a face,
> I take to reflections the deeper
> On memories far to retrace.
>
> In me have all people confided,
> The maiden her charms has displayed,
> And truths unrevealed and unuttered
> To me have been freely betrayed.

. . . .

Tho' lone in a loft I must languish
Far from closet and parlor at strife,
Content I escape from the anguish
Of the Real and the Seeming in life.[19]

The scheme of romanticism as a triad—illusion / disillusion / reconciliation—is a psychological truism. Sometimes we let simple aspects of an artist's life substitute for more difficult judgments of his work. Sometimes our own patterns get in the way; we think them evidential; and then we analyze the artist's sense of harmony. In the beginning of his career, Melville is said to have identified with Taji's suicidal quest in *Mardi*; then to have hovered between Ishmael's purgation and Ahab's cosmic defiance in *Moby-Dick;* to have expressed his mid-life bitterness in the misanthropy of *The Confidence-Man* and his ultimate Christian acceptance in the moral drama of *Billy Budd.*[20] Christian resolution of the tormenting dualism of Dostoevsky's so-called "doubles" is said to come directly from Dostoevsky's faith in Christ, and the dualism itself to proceed from the writer's own inner duality.[21]

By schematizing the fiction and pandering to the reader, simplistic biography reinforces the hegemony of the critic over the author. By dividing American painting into "Redcoatism" (inappropriate) and "Coonskinism" (appropriate), interposing an alien pattern between painting and viewer, the New York art critic Harold Rosenberg violated the art's integrity and himself controlled the viewer's response.

Independently, aesthetically, self-justifyingly, genuine art denies established reality and exposes the distance between the values of *ought to be* and the facts of *is*. At no time has that distance been greater than in the middle of the nineteenth century as the rift between scientific-materialist reality and imaginative reality widened. Physical progress through industrial production seemed a way to bend nature to human will, but the poetic mind found man's inhumanity to man unchanged, a cosmic malignancy that tainted human integrity. The nineteenth-century artist dramatized the conflict between inner self and outer world.

Many examples tie themes and styles into patterns. How intelligible the patterns are is hard to know, for the ties tend to be types or masks. Melville's masked characters either put on a mask to do evil, like bandits, or, unconsciously masked, mistake the mask for a real face. Ironically, as Miller points out, intention does not determine achievement, for the most innocent may do the greatest evil.[22] What Simmons calls Dostoevsky's "three well-defined types"—the "double," the "meek," and the "self-willed"—are fictional representations of spiritual phenomena to resolve psychological contradictions.[23] Regarded in terms of pattern, Ahab's quest becomes an allegorical agon, and each Karamazov brother embodies an attribute—Reason, Faith, Passion. One cannot say there are no such patterns, but between novelty and exactness, one may wonder which patterns matter at all. Writers are always fighting against any process that, as Stevenson said, infallibly degenerates into the cut-and-dried: "Every fresh work on which they embark is the signal for a fresh engagement of the whole forces of their mind; and the changing views which accompany the growth of their experience are marked by still more sweeping alterations in the manner of their art."[24]

The determining patterns are not psychological or religious. Even utopist ideas, such as Melville's concept of Brook Farm and Dostoevsky's participation in the Petrashevsky Circle, are tempered by social exigency. What we make of a fiction is not adequate to the artist's impulse: As we exclude aspects of a work in order to conceive the whole, so the maker was constrained by those "sweeping alterations in the manner of his art" to a partial embodiment of some original energy. Against the imperfectibility of craft comes the ideal of excellence, combining a vision of what Pater called the condition of music and some notion of merit that tradition has handed down as success and honor. Once upon a time, honor meant a good name passed from father to son, but the idea of evolutionary progress subverted the ideal of excellence. By mid-nineteenth century, more than ever before, a man's performance was measured by his accumulated property: The more he owned, the greater his power, the broader his success, and the higher his honor. Military or bureaucratic service became a means of acquiring prestige without regard to quality or value. The Socratic notion of public service as an obligation through which a citizen fulfilled part of himself and of the state as an organism of citizens became, in pluralist America and autocratic Russia, a contest between eighteenth-century values and the actual performances of conflicting interest groups, expressed vividly at the century's end by the muckrakers' revelations and the political terrorists' acts.

In the 1840s, when Dostoevsky and Melville began to write and publish, their sprawling rural societies controlled by mindless central bureaucracies were outmoded models. The drive to dominate serfs, slaves, Tartars, and redskins by bullet and by wallet had broken the old moral code, so that for Dostoevsky and Melville (unlike for Pope or Byron, for Fonvizin or Pushkin) the prevailing social order and its institutions were examples not of human potential but of human moral distortion. In his fiction each composed a microcosm in which human performance exemplified human values and a man's worth came from his heart and his hands, not from his purse.

Those "alterations in the manner of his art" made the microcosm credible. Our usual habits of understanding in terms of type or symbol or idea may seem right and formal, like an eighteenth-century view, even if we adopt Cunningham's definition of *form* as what "remains the same when everything else is changed,"[25] but they are also obstructionist. They encourage us to overlook the way innovations in style accomplish a tradition. If attitude is the way a novelist takes himself and takes his fiction, then style is the way he, in both senses, takes his time. When stories told in a new style act out the values of the past, tradition is moved forward a generation. In the end, how it is done is less significant than that it is done. Dostoevsky's style, for example, includes the "drama of the individual," interior monologue as invented early in the nineteenth century, against which, Grossman notes, he often "felt it necessary to set a somewhat officious and very precise 'auctorial' explanation, either as specific commentary or as factual information deliberately shorn of all artistic qualities."[26] Melville, for his part, sought to make interpolations "rhetorically self-sufficing," as Berthoff pointed out.[27] He sought not to imitate dramatic presentation of sentiments as carried in action but to substantiate a lyric vision by a moral scientist's observation of the things of this world. Blackmur said simply, "Melville preferred the non-dramatic mode."[28]

The social equivalents of the fictional ideals have disappeared. The Kievan Crypt Monastery, for example, which houses many martyrs' relics, is itself a relic. Only one whaling ship remains, preserved as a museum. As we look back on it, the nineteenth century may seem an era of pervasive intellectual and moral consistency much like the eighteenth, but Dostoevsky and Melville lived through two-thirds of it and saw it very differently as a period of raging social contrasts and intolerable injustice. Each posited an order to define man's elusive nature. Like every means by which men measure themselves and things, the orders were artfully made up.

2
The Hall of Mirrors

> From the beginning of the world to the present, art has always responded to man's needs and to his ideal, has always helped him in his quest for this ideal—was born with man, developed with his historical development, and died when that development ceased. . . . Creativity, the basis of art, is inseparable from man . . . and cannot have aims other than the whole man's.
>
> —*Dostoevsky*

DIVIDING TIME DRAMATICALLY BY SEQUENCE of action, not chronologically, the classic hero imposed time on place. He took all available time in the only possible place. Despite any change he experienced, any loss he suffered, the place did not change; the world around him remained stable: Achilles died, and great Troy fell, but the limits of space within which people thought were secure.

The romantic hero, on the other hand, imposed himself on eternity without concern for place. His love was sublime, the highest and most natural, an immediate expression of innate virtue, as in *Adonais,* in which differentiated neoclassic stylistic levels are brought together to recall daily, intimate life under idealized, historical circumstances. Even Mozart's diabolic Don Giovanni goes grandly to his final assignation in Hell.

A generation after Beethoven's death, man's understanding of his place in time had changed again. Industrialization had given rise to the modern city of merchant palaces and proletarian slums. From the Hellenistic period through the Middle Ages, daily life had been depicted in actual images or *figurae*, as Auerbach called them, signifying both the physical and the supraphysical, "a oneness within the divine plan of which all occurrences are parts and reflections,"[1] as gargoyles were intimate parts of beautiful cathedrals.

As commerce and manufacturing came to dominate cultural life, men stopped believing in simultaneous immediacy and sublimity. Masses of men once declared equal to others were living in squalor; their oppressors were not gods but men. Back in the classical era, men had killed and enslaved aliens, men from outside their society; in the medieval period, peasant and vassal had shared unequal reciprocity with their lord; but in the industrial era, for the first time the exploitation of the poor by the rich was built into the social base: The few owned the machinery that alienated the many. "Incentive," a euphemism for self-interest, motivated business. Money became a social agent more powerful than birth or friendship. In Russia and America, military conquest and territorial expansion shaped political and social life:

> The revival of trade after the crisis of 1847 was the dawn of a new industrial epoch. The repeal of the Corn Laws and the financial reforms subsequent thereon gave to English industry and commerce all the elbowroom they had asked for. The discovery of the Californian and Australian goldfields followed in rapid succession. The colonial markets developed at an increasing rate their capacity for absorbing English manufactured goods. In India millions of handweavers were finally crushed out by the Lancashire power-loom. China was more and more being opened up. Above all, the United States—then, commercially speaking, a mere colonial market, but by far the biggest of them all—underwent an economic development astounding even for that rapidly progressive country.[2]

Manufacturing output in America increased sixfold from 1860 to 1900, and doubled again from 1900 to 1915. In the same period, 5,300 separate firms were combined into 318 large corporations, half of which had monopoly control.[3] By 1910 half of the top business leaders had acquired their positions not through having family connections or by persisting in independent enterprise but by climbing the bureaucratic ladder. Industrial transformation of America's resources altered American society, imposed multiple standards, and reduced to hypocrisy the "self-evident truths" the eighteenth-century founders had assumed. The tripartite concept of place, space, and time changed again.

The poor lived in tenements and dreamed of Heaven. Physiological writers like Dickens, Nekrasov, and Jules Janin made verbal photographs of daily life and then superimposed a religious or a sentimental paradise, as in *A Christmas Carol,* for example, in which life's victims find comfort and love. It had nothing to do with work, with public service, or with one's deserts except morally. Dostoevsky's Edenic landscapes, as in "A Little Hero" or *Crime and Punishment,* and Melville's near paradises, as in *Typee* and *Mardi*, are alien, imagined realities. They are fantastic islands in a dream. Painted in naturalistic detail, giving authority to the relativity of cultural values, they resemble number sets with no numbers—word places where there are no readers. They are magically unreal havens for the inept but pure-in-heart, heroes like Prince Myshkin and Billy Budd who by holistic faith overcome their human failings.

Instant after instant, the "perpetual now" of photographs of poverty and alienation is unendurable. On the other hand, in the "eternal present" of a transcendent dream world does man become himself? The Renaissance heroes Hamlet and Don Quixote showed this to be impossible. By the end of the nineteenth century, when the most august social institutions that might have protected preindustrial values had become anachronistically deaf and blind (in 1895, amidst the era of the most massive monopoly formation ever, the U.S. Supreme Court declared manufacturing a local enterprise not to be treated as part of interstate commerce [*U.S. v. E.C. Knight & Co.*]), the noblest hero was Bartleby, nonconforming, nonparticipating parodist of utilitarian individualism with the macabre tag, "I would prefer not to." Whatever he did do, he did not make things worse.

"Place" also means something like Taine's *milieu,* the physical crosscurrents pressing on a man, his home in the historically material sense, ever more rapidly changed by a changing social environment. In the United States by 1840 there were 1,200 cotton factories, 1,500 woolen mills, and extensive production of ironware, armaments, tinware, clocks, shoes, and tools. In Russia, agrarianism was contracting despite the fact that under continued state militarism the land area was increasing; by 1840 there were iron and textile production, local handicrafts, and metalworking, but significant industrialization occurred in the 1880s and especially in the 1890s after expansion of the railroads two generations later than in the United States. From 1800 to 1840, both countries' populations were about 97 percent rural and 3 percent urban. Urbanization then developed rapidly in America, particularly in the Northeast. By 1900, 20 percent of the 76 million inhabitants lived in the country, 80 percent in towns. In Russia, the ratio remained reversed; of 130 million people, nearly 90 percent still lived in the country, only 10 percent in towns. America was on the move, as the slogan says, its population growing at a rate double that of Russia's, and its cities growing three times as fast as the total population. Melville and most of the men in his family for several generations were involved in the maritime commerce on which the population explosion and economic development depended. Dostoevsky's father was an army doctor; Dostoevsky was trained as a military engineer.

In Russia, religious orthodoxy discouraged economic change and repressed dissent. In America, years before the Civil War, Calvinist enthusiasm sponsored business enterprise and the abolition of slavery, giving rise to an original social amalgam, which Tocqueville noticed. "When an individual or a party is wrong in the United States," he asked,

> to whom can he apply for redress? If to public opinion, public opinion constitutes the majority; if to the legislature, it represents the majority and implicitly obeys it; if to the executive power, it is appointed by the majority and serves as a passive tool in its hands. The public force consists of the majority under arms; the jury is the majority invested with the right of hearing judicial cases; and in certain states even the judges are elected by the majority. However iniquitous or absurd the measure of which you complain, you must submit to it as well as you can. . . . By this means habits are formed in the heart of a free country which may some day prove fatal to its liberties.[4]

"Any man more right than his neighbors," Thoreau claimed in defiant civil disobedience, "constitutes a majority of one already."[5]

Derivatively European, expansionist, and militaristic, both America and Russia were truculently Christian. Each had a literary champion advancing an antiestablishment ideal of the common good—Whitman and Nekrasov. Whitman, poet and newspaperman much admired by Melville, celebrated the spirit of open change, declared that American workers and farmers were a majority with political power. Nekrasov, poet and editor of *Sovremennik* (The Contemporary), first publisher of Dostoevsky, praised the virtues of the peasants, a majority that had no power. Because both poets were inventive craftsmen and because they lauded romantic aspects of national character, both became venerated national poets, but in his popular work each omitted harsh facts that he knew. Whitman nursed soldiers during the Civil War, and Nekrasov wrote innovative studies of the Petersburg slums. Both believed in social reform; even their nostalgic verse had a hortatory tone.

Despite their idealism and early political dissidence, Dostoevsky and Melville in their work present society as unredeemable. Their different but coherent views suppose facts of social life to be terminal and unalterable. Until man by his own free will changes his nature, nothing can change the nature of his world. In the mid-1870s, in the society of *Anna Karenina,* in which Vronsky rides steeplechases, the Bolkonskys give balls, and Stiva and Levin shoot woodcock, the poor lived as they had for hundreds of years. As Nekrasov had described them in the late 1830s, so Dostoevsky depicts them in the 1870s: "Where he [the boy] came from, it was pitch-black at night; there was only one light on the whole street. The little low wooden houses were all shuttered. The moment it grew dark, nobody was on the streets; everyone locked himself indoors. There were only packs of howling dogs, hundreds and thousands of them, wailing and barking all night." The boy's mother had died in the basement corner where they lived. The boy wanders out, sees the holiday crowds and other children's parties, starves, freezes to death, and joins the blessed children around Christ's Christmas tree: "They all are here now, all like angels, all with Christ, and He Himself is in their midst, holding His hands out to them and blessing them and their sinful mothers. And all the mothers stand to one side and weep. Each recognizes her boy or girl, and the children fly to them and kiss them and wipe away their tears with their little hands and beg them not to cry, because they are so happy here."[6]

Brief and simple, "The Boy at Christ's Christmas Party" assumes gross class distinctions and, as part of Dostoevsky's *A Writer's Diary,* argues that the poor are cruelly exploited and that exploitation cannot be rationalized. If one innocent child suffers—that is, is displaced—the whole system is wrong. In the story, as in life, social selfishness kills the boy, but the boy's death does not affect the system: "In the morning the yardman found the little corpse of a boy who had run in behind the woodpile and frozen to death. They searched and found his mama, too. . . . She had died even before he had. The two of them met again with God up in Heaven."

In that other world, intimately and spiritually connected to this, there is room. To know your place in this world means to suffer injustice, something no institution can compensate or remedy. Your real place shows up in faith's picture, lies there in faith's substance. That world includes everyone. It is a cohesive view, giving depth and intellectual structure to all of Dostoevsky's work.

Melville's quarrel with civilization begins in *Typee* and runs through his work, directed especially at the inconsistencies of religion. The very title of "The Paradise of Bachelors and the Tartarus of Maids," about a dinner in the Temple, London, and a visit to a New England paper mill, points it out. Melville underscored his basic lifelong attitude by underlining in Shelley's *Works:*

> *Me,* who am as a nerve o'er which do creep
> The else-unfelt oppressions of this earth.[7]

Next to the fulsome passage in Emerson's *Essays* about the sailor's life renewing itself in storm as in calm, he wrote, "To one who has weathered Cape Horn as a common sailor what stuff all this is."[8]

Unmasking the rich man's satiety opens "The Paradise of Bachelors" with the arresting alliteration of calculated rhetoric: "Sweet are the oases in Sahara; charming the isle-groves of August prairies; delectable pure faith amidst a thousand perfidies: but sweeter, still more charming, most delectable, the dreamy Paradise of Bachelors, found in the stony heart of stunning London."[9]

To Melville's way of thinking, the displacements are always grotesque—allegorically simple exaggerations of an untenable claim. Hell is the distortions caused by work and pain; Heaven is the irony of satisfaction, made clear in summary description of the Temple, "indeed a city by itself. A city with all the best appurtenances, as the above enumeration shows. A city with a park to it, and flower-beds, and a river-side—the Thames flowing by as openly, in one part, as by Eden's primal garden flowed the mild Euphrates. In what is now the Temple Garden the old Crusaders used to exercise their steeds and lances; the modern Templars now lounge on the bench beneath the trees, and, switching their patent-leather boots, in gay discourse exercise at repartee."[10]

The argument by inflated parallel, undercut by parenthetical put-down, is persuasive: Eden's pleasures are alluring but pretentious. In themselves they are harmless, perhaps ridiculous. The images that build the false heaven become its reshaping metaphors. For example, the Temple complex of rooms and lawyers' offices is finally called a cheese. The apartment where the nine bachelors dine is well up toward Heaven to make the guests work up an appetite. As the whales in *Moby-Dick* are likened to "a mob of young collegians . . . tumbling round the world" and then to a Turkish harem, a parody of the game men hunt, so the diners do not simply begin dinner but get "fairly under way."[11] After several courses, "the heavy artillery of the feast marched in, led by that well-known English generalissimo, roast beef." The whole meal becomes a mock engagement: The waiter is called a field marshal; his head is said to resemble Socrates'. Rabelaisian sport continues until the battle is won. Pain and trouble do not exist—"Such monkish fables can't be." All in a "decorum unassailable by any degree of mirthfulness," save the author's whose last comic fillip is that after dinner some diners go "to their neighbouring chambers to turn over the *Decameron* ere retiring for the night"—another caustic definition of their distance from passion and from pain.

The other half of the tale is a first-person narrative by a seedsman of his wagon trip with his horse Black past Woedolor Mountain through Black Notch down to a paper mill in Devil's Dungeon on Blood River:

> When upon reining up at the protruding rock I at last caught sight of the quaint groupings of the factory-buildings and with the travelled highway and the Notch behind, found myself all alone, silently and privily stealing through deep-cloven passages into this sequestered spot, and saw the long, high-gabled main factory edifice, with a rude tower—for hoisting heavy boxes—at one end, standing among its crowded outbuildings and boarding-houses, as the Temple Church amidst the surrounding offices and dormitories, and when the marvellous retirement of this mysterious mountain nook fastened its whole spell upon me, then, what memory lacked, all tributary imagination furnished, and I said to myself, "This is the very counterpart of the Paradise of Bachelors, but snowed upon, and frost-painted to a sepulchre."[12]

Sexual allegory overtakes the Latinate rhetoric; alliteration becomes an identifying rhythm; and sympathy shifts from the figures of absurdity to their victims. The rosy paper manufactured accentuates the whiteness of the factory girls:

> Not a syllable was breathed. Nothing was heard but the low, steady, overruling hum of the iron animals. The human voice was banished from the spot. Machinery—that vaunted slave of humanity—here stood menially served by human beings, who served mutely and cringingly as the slave serves the Sultan. The girls did not so much seem accessory wheels to the general machinery as mere cogs to the wheels. . . .
>
> "You find it rather stifling here," coughed I in answer; "but the girls don't cough."
>
> "Oh, they are used to it."
>
> "Where do you get such hosts of rags?" picking up a handful from a basket.
>
> "Some from the country round about; some from far over sea—Leghorn and London."
>
> "'Tis not unlikely then," murmured I, "that among these heaps of rags there may be some old shirts, gathered from the dormitories of the Paradise of Bachelors. But the buttons are all dropped off. Pray, my lad, do you ever find any bachelor's buttons hereabouts?"[13]

Through the rest of the sketch, the two-tiered allegory—for example, buttons equal semen—is explicit, and the paronomasia, precritical—"I suppose the handling of such white bits of sheets all the time makes them so sheety"—but the account is powerful and exemplifies Melville's sense of the grotesque within the grand style. Like drones, the bachelors live their ludicrous redundancy off the maids' labor, returning nothing. Their indifference heightens the terrifying injustice. Equilibrium is found only in comedic artifice—"It is colder here [in Devil's Dungeon] than at the top of Woedolor Mountain"—that, as in *The Divine Comedy,* presents a unified view of man's distortions. Everyone is out of place: The women should not be slaves; the factory should not be a dungeon; and no man should be a parasite. But who will change? The displacements are beyond the author's repair. Under the perceptions of absurdity lie terror and pity.

Dostoevsky's grotesque is suppler, funnier, more inventive, even whimsical. Gibian has listed a half-dozen functional aspects of it: It is a form of dissent by the impotent; it creates scandal; it blends the real and the fantastic, enhancing the realism; it introduces themes obversely; it presents distortions antithetical to oversimplification.[14] Most of these are found in the story "Another Man's Wife and the Husband under the Bed," in which a man crawls under a woman's bed at her husband's approach only to find another man already there. Both have mistaken the apartment anyway:

> "Shut up!"
> "Sir! You're forgetting yourself. You have no idea who you're talking to!"
> "To a gentleman who's lying under a bed."
> "But I was caught by surprise—a mistake. Whereas you, if I'm not mistaken, came for immoral purposes."
> "You're very much mistaken."
> "Sir! I'm older than you, as I've told you—"
> "Sir! Realize that we're in the same boat. Please don't poke me in the face."
> "Sir! I'm not poking anything. Excuse me, but there's no room."
> "Why are you so fat?"
> "Lord, I've never been in such a lowdown position."
> "True, you can't lie down any lower."[15]

The sentences make a routine; the routine becomes a farce: No man could have gotten into the lady's bed, for (*a*) she was faithfully married, as prevailing morals required, and (*b*) as comic convention demands, she preferred her little dog. Alas, the dog awakes in its corner, scents the men, with a yelp scurries under the bed. In panic, Ivan Andreyevich throttles it. Comic confusion: The younger man flees; Ivan Andreyevich goes through a vaudeville of apology to the husband; the wife weeps and screams that he murdered her little dog. Ivan Andreyevich, who, in fact, was jealously trying to catch his own wife with a lover, argues that he couldn't have been seeking the lady, for her lover must be a Richardson or a Lovelace. That caps the self-mockery. The lady bursts into delighted laughter. The husband is mollified. The quasi-literary allusion puts everything in place. The wife turns to her husband: "Sweetie, he can't be a thief, but how did he get in?" Ivan Andreyevich says that it is as strange as fiction and then digresses from his explanation to offer the lady a new little dog "that eats only sugar." At home, he finds his wife in bed with toothache, and he begins explaining all over again: "Sweetie, sweetie . . . ." These are the silly, superficial members of a middle-class paradise who, out of selfish uninterestedness, oppress the poor and pervert Christian values. Their craving for material satisfaction is sentimental and ridiculous. In their absurdity, they do not even suppose that a boy at Christ's Christmas party exists.

Melville's comic spirit, drawing on the sea literature of his time, learned from Shakespeare to combine reflections on mortality and experiences of absurdity. The "great moments" of cosmic catastrophe are glued-up and bronze-fastened by comic contradictions. As Hamlet re-creates himself talking to Yorick's skull, so Ishmael finds salvation on a coffin. Gloucester puns on Edmund's birth; Ishmael comments about a sailor in the New Bedford inn carving on a settle, "He was trying his hand at a ship under full sail, but he didn't make much headway, I thought."[16] "How bitter a thing it is to look into happiness through another man's eyes!" says

Orlando in *As You Like It.* "Plagiarize otherwise as they may, not often are the men of this world plagiarists in praise," says Ford, the narrator of "Jimmy Rose." Rabelaisian and Dickensian in meaningful levity is Ishmael's argument that "hell is an idea first born on an undigested apple-dumpling." Bright, bawdy puns often make ordinary speech intelligible. The landlord tells Ishmael that Queequeg is "an early bird—airley to bed and airley to rise—yes, he's the bird what catches the worm."[17] The landlord's pleasure in his own wit points up by his ignorance of philosophy and his lack of experience with whales the vastness of the quest, the fatality of pursuit, and the tragedy of conflict.

Dostoevsky's Christian faith precludes cosmic despair. Dull men riding their hobbyhorses become, like Gogol's cardboard figures, ridiculous not out of high-minded service to an obsolete ideal, like Quixote, but out of witless repetition. Ptitsyn in *The Idiot* is a decently educated, decently dressed, decently intentioned man "with no ideas of his own" who, like Pirogov in Gogol's "Nevsky Prospect," becomes the harmless but vulgar victim of his own "effrontery of naïveté." Others' comicality derives from their trying to act out such lives that people will not see who they are or discover the disparity between their ideals and their absurdities. By trying to follow "normal" patterns, they conceal their grotesqueness from other characters but expose it to the reader. For example, Raskolnikov feels that he is grotesque, but he does not know that his hat labels him. He fears people think him ridiculous, but he cannot tell how ridiculously he behaves.

In the early tales, Dostoevsky achieved comic effects by parodying other works and by mocking his own characters, playing games with literary conventions and increasing the intellectual content of the fiction. In the later tales, his style dramatized the self-consciousness of absurdity, delving into each character's individuality. In *Notes from the Cellar,* provisionally titled "A Confession," the lyric complaint of a lonely man begging for unacknowledgeable sympathy becomes an unusable ratio about self-knowledge. In *The Idiot,* Nastasya Filippovna argues against Myshkin, who supports her, but denies the world, which condemns her. Like the Man in the Cellar, she argues with a projection of herself. In *Crime and Punishment,* Raskolnikov actually addresses himself in the second person singular; then for him, as for Ippolit in *The Idiot,* the expected end turns into its own distortion, after which comes the unfunny office of faith. Talking to Aglaya about Ippolit's attempted suicide or to Nastasya Filippovna about herself, Myshkin is a deputy of love who penetrates other people's debates with their dramatized selves. In *The Demons,* Tikhon cuts into Stavrogin's exorcising his conscience on the grounds of style: He points out that Stavrogin beforehand fears and hates the very people whom he needs for his confession, that he fears and hates the very self he loves and finds mysterious. There is no "humor" here, but the absurdity prevents tragedy. Ivan Karamazov's madness prevents resolution of the debate between his cynical, ironic, sophisticated self and the servile, mimicking, insinuating voice of Smerdyakov. The conflict between the "I" and the "other" is ridiculous because it cannot be harmonized except in the constructs of fiction where the fantastic, too, is real.

The vision of emancipation, dignity, and ease that theories of social progress promised and to which the dissident Dostoevsky and Melville believed mankind should be heading was perverted by human cupidity, bad luck, and the very structure of the world itself. True, a man's worldview is in many ways a magic-lantern projection of his own psychological state, but it is as "real" as any other comprehensive scheme for ordering experience. A literary failure after *Pierre*, a dualistic ironist who found evil lurking in good and good rising out of evil, an allegorical naturalist, Melville experienced and interpreted the Holy Land as an insoluble Problem of Good and Evil set in a desert of Loss. He jotted down in his journal,

> Ride over mouldy plain to Dead Sea—Mountains on their side—Lake George—all but verdure.—foam on beach & pebbles like slaver of mad dog—smarting bitter of the water,—carried the bitter in my mouth all day—bitterness of life—thought of all bitter things—Bitter is it to be poor & bitter, to be reviled, & Oh bitter are these waters of Death, thought I.—Old boughs tossed up by water—relics of pick-nick—nought to eat but bitumen & ashes with desert of Sodom apples washed down with water of Dead Sea.—Must bring your own provisions, as well, too, for mind as body—for all is barren.[18]

For Dostoevsky, the vision lay beyond the border of man's corrupt world, something between an oasis and a mirage. He painted a picture of it in "A Little Hero":

> The sun had risen high and floated splendidly above us through the deep, dark blue sky, melting, it seemed, in its own fire. The reapers had already moved far on. They could hardly be seen from our side. Behind them, the endless rows of mown grass crept constantly on, and every so often a light breeze stirred gently and blew the fragrant aroma over to us. All around was the incessant concert of those who "do not reap, neither do they sow" but are as free as the air cut by their dallying wings. It seemed that in that moment each flower, each least blade of grass, smoking with the odor of sacrifice, was saying to its Creator, "Father! I'm blissful and happy!"[19]

Intolerable, inexplicable contradictions in the actual world so disturbed Dostoevsky and Melville, who thought within a Christian framework of transcendental values, that they had to invent an artistically expressive, recognizably human society complete, functional, and proper—not a pompous allegory or passing whim or clever parody, but a coherent structure embracing the extremes of human behavior—through which they could propose transforming individual evil and general corruption into moral and common good. It had to be a perfectible fiction allusively real, a yardstick for measuring performance against capacity, manner against tradition. It had to be a moral microcosm reflecting and evaluating change. It had to celebrate excellence and enforce a theory of justice. For Melville, it was the ship; for Dostoevsky, the monastery.

3
The Labyrinth

> Art in the long run is as good a measure of honesty as we have; moving in the actual, it plays on truth.
>
> —*Blackmur*

IN 1958, UNDER THE INFLUENCE OF JUNG'S *Modern Man in Search of a Soul,* a critic analyzed *Crime and Punishment* through the number four: "The number four has archetypal significance, for it is an aspect of the cosmic universe."[1] In 1975, a French critic, believing in man's soul as the battleground between God and Satan and in *l'éternel retour,* "deciphered" *Moby-Dick*: "The magic square of 16 is the very structure of the book."[2] Pleasant are the delusions of firm answers in matters subject to rereadings and revision, but imposing plain, generic patterns obscures what the author even had in mind. No rigid interpretation accounts for deviations. Texture and tension, surface coloring and the play among words' references and words' suggestions, like rhythm in verse, are built by offering and declining a norm. In the epilogue to *War and Peace,* Tolstoy said that men can no more explain historical events than they can explain electricity: "Atoms attract, atoms repel each other. . . . If every man has free will, that is, if every man can act as he desires, then all history is a series of unconnected accidents. . . . The greater the perceived role of necessity, the smaller the role of freedom. And vice versa." Because the historian considers what is known, subject to the laws of necessity and what is unknown, free, his conception of freedom "is merely an expression of the unknown remainder of what we know about the laws of human life." To admit that men have free will and can exercise it in historical circumstances—that is, can act not subject to the laws of necessity—is to destroy the possibility of history: "If there exists but one free-willed human act, then there is not a single historical law and no concept of historical events."[3]

Historians summarize or codify after the fact, but they do not describe what actually happens as men experience it, and they cannot predict. Similarly, pattern makers substitute intellectual structure for aesthetic. They give in to the temptation to resolve the dilemmas of ambiguity by intellectualization or classification. From the artist's point of view, they cheat by building a superficial labyrinth.

Melville expressed irreducible contradictions. In *Mardi*, he equated intelligence with spiritual love: "Right reason, and Alma, are the same; else Alma, not reason, would we reject. The Master's great command is Love; and here do all things wise, and all things good, unite."[4] On the other hand, implicitly in his longer works and explicitly in some unfinished pieces, he satirized God, faith, religiosity, and the loyalty that puts others ahead of self. Bernard Shaw later treated God as an avuncular humbug, but Melville took theology so personally that he assumed a force of evil equivalent to the idea of good. God cannot be conceived without the Devil, he says in Manichean spirit, because "madness is undefinable. It & right reason extremes of one."[5] In "Roast Beef in the Pulpit," he notes that "it is better to laugh & not sin than to weep & be wicked." A man's proper introduction into the world is sanctioned not by God but by the Devil: "Ego non baptizo te in nomine Patris et Filii et Spiritus Sancti—sed in nomine Diaboli."[6] As Melville saw it, this is the cosmic joke that God plays on every man. It is the basis of the human conspiracy in melancholy, corruption, and vengeance.

There are a number of borders to this fiction. Dillingham lists some in his study of "Cock-A-Doodle-Doo!"—Melville's narrative of a search for a fantastic cock. Some critics characterize the story as a parody; some define it as an optimistic allegory; Dillingham finds it autobiographical: "Through self-glorification the narrator overcomes his fears of emasculation, of the consequences of worldly failure and, finally, of death."[7] All—and none—of the interpretations seem apt. Especially because "Cock-A-Doodle-Doo!" does not lift off from Melville's intentions, does not become self-sufficient fiction, it exposes the antagonism between Melville and the world: "This toiling posture brought my head pretty well earthward, as if I were in the act of butting it against the world. I marked the fact, but only grinned at it with a ghastly grin."[8] It also exposes his longing for a means of establishing equilibrium between the commerce that runs the world and the religious values by which men are good or bad: "A miserable world! Who would take the trouble to make a fortune in it, when he knows not how long he can keep it. . . . Great improvements of the age! What! to call the facilitation of death and murder [by train accident] an improvement! Who wants to travel so fast? My grandfather did not, and he was no fool."[9]

A past age regarded from a distance seems harmonious; our grandfathers' time invariably seems stronger and better than ours. We live in the present, as they once did—on the edge of time. But as Melville saw things, nineteenth-century efforts to conquer space and time were dangerously out of control.

Melville's bind was the impossibility of reconciling "progress" with "that old-time religion," the dominant socioeconomic and intellectual forces of a world becoming more and more "American" and middle-class. He could not blinker either. He felt he had to find some way of housing his melancholy despite the unending incongruities he perceived and the injustice he experienced. Wisdom seemed more tempting than love. In any case, he always perceived contraries. The only pattern that seems to hold for all his work is the literarily ironic, in which opposites are presented simultaneously attracting and repelling each other. Even what seems to have been the foundation for his value judgments and his morality, mankind's ultimate goodness, is denied. In "Bartleby, the Scrivener," for example, he presents the moral confusion of Christ returned as the least significant man. From inertia, the world's headlong rush is more than anyone can check. The facts mock, then destroy the values. Melville's "parable teaches one thing clearly," according to Fiene, "that when Christ returns as the Messiah we shall deny him and betray him and crucify him again."[10] The power that makes Melville's prose seem dramatic, though not in the dramatic mode, comes from the scrupulousness with which he presented the time-space dilemma. Caught between the past and the future, the artist is condemned to the ever-perishing present.

Dostoevsky tries to duck it by repeatedly choosing love over wisdom and by asserting that the Agent of Love would naturally come to those who need him. "The Russian people have always suffered like Christ," says Sonya in Dostoevsky's notebooks. "We are God's children; we live in Hell. There is one, Christ. He took pity on everyone." A moment later she adds, "Whoever is living . . . *if he is really alive,* then he suffers, and consequently he needs Christ, and consequently Christ will come."[11] Man's spiritual search and the spiritual essence that unites him with his god are analogous to the artist's quest and the artistic essence. Why, Dostoevsky asked, does artistic creativity "become an idol to be worshipped? Because the need for beauty is most developed when man is in opposition to actuality, out of harmony with it, struggling against it, that is, when *he is most alive,* because man is most alive precisely when he seeks something and is in the process of getting it. Then there comes out the most natural desire for all things harmonious, for tranquility, and in beauty there are both harmony and tranquility."[12]

His novels treat men as they would be rewarded and as they appear. "The theme of *The Idiot* is the inadequacy of mere goodness in the world of today," wrote Lesser.[13] Inasmuch as to be alive is to suffer, consciousness is a degree of anguish. Anguish is a characteristic of the elite, those intelligent enough to know that they suffer, whose defenses against suffering, like the Grand Inquisitor's, are carefully, cynically elaborated. The more firmly a man posits an exclusively materialistic world, the more vehemently he asserts that progress is to be made by ever greater exploitation of nature and of men. He does not internalize his values but, like Napoleon and Baron von Rothschild, materializes his idea.

On the other hand, he who believes that man's nature is not adequately described by the matter on which it works must rebel against the tyranny of the majority for no "good reason." Like Raskolnikov, he will fail. His rebellion will be rational in the name of old values, but altered social conditions will render it inappropriate. Any rebellion to establish justice must fail because of its self-contradictory anachronisms. The need for revolution arises when the agencies of the present, out of control according to traditional values, intolerably repress the majority of those who have social power, but the absence of values means that the revolution, too, like any other set of acts, must be inappropriate.

In *Sentimental Education,* Flaubert typified the stages and the points of view, reserving disinterested judgment to himself. Either the revolutionary actor suffers death (failure), or he becomes an artist. The most he can do, Dostoevsky suggests, is evaluate his effort in terms of beauty's size and order. Then his "real" failure is not that he did not do what he intended but that, like Raskolnikov, he failed aesthetically. Raskolnikov does not fear violence, and his double murder makes clear that he would agree with convicts like Jack Abbott, who declared that the man who fears violence loses himself as a man.[14] Ironically, Raskolnikov commits violent crime without advocating violence. Protesting, he accepts the external duality, but that causes internal ambivalence. No matter how he moves, he knows that he is simultaneously right and wrong.

Augustine wrote that "either there is evil which we fear, or the fact that we fear is evil. . . . [I examined] an idea I had heard—namely that our free-will is the cause of our doing evil. . . . I was quite certain that it was myself and no other who willed, and I came to see that the cause of my sin lay there."[15] Source of fictional motive and ethical judgment, free will is the exclusive and powerful agent that transforms human life. When charged with madness by his friends, Don Quixote replied that he knew very well who he was and also what he could be. By taking responsibility for himself, he asserted freedom. As Melville put it in *Mardi,* "Within our hearts is all we seek."

But the power that can liberate can destroy. In art, if an

individual cannot transform the values by which he is defined, any attempt at transcendence by violence or by rebellion against the established materialism will lead to his death. Kirillov in *The Demons* truthfully completes his fake confession with the ironic "Liberté, égalité, fraternité ou la mort!"

Melville denies that man can escape evil. Evil is universal. Repressed in one place, it erupts in another. It is not so much a principle as a condition—or a characteristic of a condition. He says that the force of evil underlies and overshadows human life. Despite evil's effects, understanding of evil helps explain the world. In fact, such understanding makes life meaningful: Greater than love is the moral knowledge of control. "This great power of blackness in him [Hawthorne]," Melville wrote, "derives its force from its appeals to that Calvinistic sense of Innate Depravity and Original Sin, from whose visitations, in some shape or other, no deeply thinking mind is always and wholly free. For, in certain moods, no man can weigh this world without throwing in something, somehow like Original Sin, to strike the uneven balance."[16]

Laid out on a page, Dostoevsky's anthropocentric view of man is schematic: The Devil and God wait patiently seated on opposite ends of a seesaw while men in a hundred costumes—the Man in the Cellar, the Grand Inquisitor, Prince "Mouse"—battle for the right to tip the balance. Only otherworldly characters, vessels of divine love like Sonya, see the two splayed arms underneath, holding up the seesaw. Christ, the living Savior-Sufferer, has replaced Atlas. Not physical levers but spiritual love supports the world. Or as the Man in the Cellar dramatizes, the burden of freedom is the seed of death. In *A Writer's Diary,* Dostoevsky comments, "Every *great* happiness contains some suffering, for it gives rise to greater consciousness."[17] In *The Demons,* Zosima says that life rightly comprehended is paradise. Meanwhile, according to a much-quoted line from *The Karamazov Brothers,* "the devil wars with god, and the battlefield is the human heart."

Dostoevsky partially revives the romantic point of view. The notion that he who finds what he seeks in the struggle against the conditions of life becomes sick with ennui (*acedia*) and grotesquely exaggerates his craving is like the three stages of the romantic mood: idealistic illusion, worldly disillusion, ironic or parodic reconciliation. Dostoevsky considered *acedia* morally self-destructive. Like the modern, worldly religious poet Anthony Hecht, we, too, think that much comfort ruins the muscles, that laziness is intellectually self-destructive:

> The first man leaps the ditch. (Who wins this race
> Wins laurel, but laurel dies.)
> The next falls in (who in his hour of grace
> Plucked out his offending eyes.)
> The blind still lead. (Consider the ant's way;
> Consider, and be wise.)[18]

Separated from the novels, Dostoevsky's ideas seem overripe borrowings from European philosophy and literature. The ideas and opinions he put forth in his essays now appear conservative, belligerently nationalistic, even dishonest, in large part contrary to his experience. For example, few Russians now believe that the Russian people are the essence of purity and tolerance.[19] Most of Dostoevsky's pronouncements seem polemical efforts to persuade himself or to advance a cause. He well knew that Russian peasants and workers were ill-fed, ill-housed, and ill-clothed, but he declared that art was as necessary to man as food and drink. All his life, middle-class Dostoevsky resented receiving less money for his writing than nobly born Tolstoy, and he despised middle-class materialism and mannerisms. Nevertheless he wrote that "man seeks art, finds and accepts the beautiful *without any limiting conditions,* merely because it is beautiful, reverentially bows down to it without asking what it is good for or how much it can buy."[20]

Insightful and prophetic, vain and more zealously missionary than most writers, he was a dynamo of contrasts, and his mind was too large to trip over a foolish inconsistency. When he said that "art is always contemporary and actual, has never been otherwise and cannot be,"[21] I think he meant that the delight of art is the impossibility of escaping its dilemma. Embodied in art, an idea comes alive with all its human tenacity and ambiguity. We learn to follow patterned movement without restricting ourselves to what it "means," as most people find aesthetic pleasure in their existence with others, especially in large cities full of sounds, color, and motion. "It would seem that the exciting and invigorating power of this participation in mass life," Milosz wrote even after the Second World War, "springs from the feeling of *potentiality,* of constant unexpectedness, of a mystery one ever pursues."[22] Or as Dreiser commented in the opening paragraph of chapter 30 of *Sister Carrie,* "In New York the roads were any one of a half-hundred, and each had been diligently pursued by hundreds, so that celebrities were numerous. The sea was already full of whales."

A nation lives not by bread and manufactured goods, Dostoevsky said, but "by the ideas which nourish its heart and soul. . . . The Germans have attained the heights of political status."[23] In the name of cultural unity and national pride he advocated a Slavic community under Russian power at the expense of the Poles, the Czechs, and the South Slavs: "For political, governmental and other such reasons, the Tartars must be expelled and Russians settled on their land."[24] He supported the government's war against the Turks in 1877–78 and "prophesied" the Russian capture of Byzantium, basing his argument on the moral grounds that only by returning to the seat of Orthodoxy could the Russians achieve their ideal of embracing all humanity in the spirit and faith of Christ. Evil he believed (1) the result of sloppy workmanship or (2) eschatologically man's perfect self-perversion. Perseveringly, in the last years of his life he preached Orthodox Christianity. Christ's communistic way—"Anyone who wishes to be a follower of mine must leave self behind; he must take up his cross, and come with me. Whoever cares for his own safety is lost; but if a man will let himself be lost for my sake and for the Gospel, that man is safe"[25]—was what Dostoevsky believed in, unconnected to his version of the Slavophile tradition and state Orthodoxy. Dostoevsky's exhortations combined excessive ambition, moral fervor, and political ineptitude. He thought he had more political-polemical clout than he had. Some intellectuals, however, took him seriously, like Lev Shestov: "He terrified us by prophesying that Europe would be drenched in rivers of blood because of the warfare between the classes, while in Russia, thanks to our Russian ideal of universal humanity, not only would our internal problems be peacefully solved but also a new, unheard-of word would be found whereby we would save hapless Europe. A quarter of a century has passed. But we ourselves are drowning, literally drowning ourselves, in blood."[26]

Even in Shestov's mirror we see that Dostoevsky's criteria for saving Europe were aesthetic. Young Verkhovensky in

The Demons is both a nihilist—one who, according to Dostoevsky, can see only material goals, not artistic harmonies—and a lover of beauty. In *The Karamazov Brothers,* Dmitry says, "Beauty is a terrifying and awful thing. . . . In it the borders come together; all contradictions are contained in it. . . . What's terrifying is that what to the intellect seems disgraceful to the heart seems purely beautiful."[27] Dostoevsky's personae argue that "beauty will save the world," but the arguments, like the ideas themselves, are ancillary to the fiction. By persuading himself of their dramatic truth, he justified the urgency of his work, and by persuading others to save the world for beauty, he won his work the room it needed.

What are considered conflicting ideas in his work are dramatic, but they are not strictly dilemmas. To defend them as dilemmas, one must first assume Dostoevsky's polarized definition of man. A logical schema for a dilemma[28]—

$$\begin{array}{l} a \vee b \\ a \supset c \\ b \supset d \\ \hline c \vee d \end{array}$$

—filled with condensations of Dostoevsky's ideas would look like this:

A man can live in society either by the principles of reason or by the spirit of love.

If he lives by principles of reason, he will be in danger of losing his individuality and his ability to accept love.

If he lives by the spirit of love, he will be in danger of being sacrificed to the power of society.

> A man in society either will lose his individuality or will be overwhelmed by social pressure.

Dostoevsky's argument has been reduced to the horns of the dilemma, each of which is detrimental to his original position but which he accepts as the basis for dramatic conflict among his characters. As Dmitry must choose between public disgrace and private ecstasy, Dostoevsky must choose between two "evils"—evil because partial. What is good because whole Dostoevsky calls the *xudožestvennost'* of a literary work, what the dictionary labels "high artistic value," what Aristotle called the "ordering of the pattern," what we think of as the sense of style.

We return to it when we see what the borders coming together gather in their net. In *Notes from the Dead House,* for example, the horrible and the risible are combined without distortion: "Despite all possible points of view, everybody will agree that there are certain crimes which, always and everywhere, according to any possible law, have, since the world began, been considered indisputable crimes and will be so considered as long as man is man. Only in prison did I hear stories about the most horrible, most unnatural acts, the most monstrous murders, told with the most irrepressible, almost childlike, gay laughter."[29] Marlowe's *Doctor Faustus,* Goethe's *Faust,* Ansky's *The Dybbuk*—there is a long line of literary representations of a world where the Devil is in charge.

Freud's *Interpretation of Dreams* has as epigraph a line from the *Aeneid: Flectere si nequeo superos, Acheronta movebo,* which means "If I cannot persuade the gods above, I will move the region of the Acheron," or as Day Lewis has translated it:

> Well, if my powers are not great enough,
> I shall not hesitate—that's sure—to ask help wherever
> Help may be found. If the gods above are no use to me, then I'll
> Move all hell.[30]

In such manner, says Freud, the material suppressed by the superego forces itself into consciousness in dreams. If God is the repressive superego, the Devil is the permissive superego. "The pact with the Devil," Roheim notes, "is therefore really a pact with the Super-Ego not to help human beings in getting those things but to stop preventing them in doing so."[31]

The next analytical step is to rebel against the suppression, that is, to unmask the dream content. It is conscious rebellion, an avowed revolt. For that, Dostoevsky and Melville knew, you do need the Devil's help.

4
Fact into Fiction

> The transformation of actuality around us depends on its transformation inside us; creativity is more basic than cognition.
>
> —*Bely*

PHILOSOPHICAL VALUES SEEM TO INFLUENCE the uses of the environment more than environmental changes affect values. In the history of New York harbor, for example, technology expressing mercantile, aggressive values for three hundred years turned an Indian canoe-landing into an ever busier port, but twenty-five years after the collapse of shipping, the harbor polluted, and one-third of the city's drinking water on the verge of being unpotable, those commercial values lean even more on technology and are even more aggressive. Differences between the native Manhattoes and the seventeenth-century Dutchmen who bought their island—as between the Tahitians and Marquesans, on the one hand, and the nineteenth-century English and French colonialists on the other—argue for a cultural relativism almost inconceivable before the twentieth century.

The idea that all men at all times in all places have similar natures was a Renaissance idea believed by Melville's hero Montaigne, for whom men were alike both in their divine potential and in their devilish individuality. But Melville did not regard himself as a model. At most, he was a sympathetic observer who played hide-and-seek with his readers, assuming that no common system held men together but that "if you rightly look for it, you will almost always find that the author himself has somewhere furnished you with his own picture."[1] In old-fashioned, grand canvases, eschewing popular romance and grappling with ontological questions, he, like Dostoevsky, entered his fiction as a psychological investment in his principal characters or as an undistinguished, almost invisible reporter (Ishmael in *Moby-Dick,* Mr. G-v in *The Demons*) to introduce the characters and to offer eyewitness accounts and then, like the classic chorus, to slip offstage.

Insofar as the life of civilized man has been characterized by prevailing scarcity, control of the environment and the transformation of nature have made his life materially easier. From technological invention have come cultural changes augmenting desire and encouraging expressiveness. The more popular these inventions, like cars and television sets, the more social barriers have broken down and the more taboos have disappeared. Certainly, the engines of industry exploited human labor, and the steam press brought about the penny paper and pulp fiction. The rise of mass culture in the 1840s and competition for control of that market titillated workers' dreams of a land of milk and honey, sunshine and free love begun by the discovery of Tahiti in 1767. In France, Bougainville's first reports supported Rousseau's ideas and became part of the cry for reform that led to the Revolution. In England, Cook's voyages occasioned some scientific experiments (such as trying to measure the transit of Venus) and some unsuccessful missionary activity, but to the popular mind they presented pictures of a living Garden of Eden. In America, the explorers' accounts were augmented by tales of whaling voyages. Melville's early, exotic, suggestively erotic romances, though neither prudish nor exploitative, satisfied this yearning and were financially successful.

The aristocratic 1820s of Melville's childhood had gone. Discharged from the navy in 1844, Melville was caught in a double bind between two worlds—the seemingly gracious, high-minded past and the frenetic present; Polynesian communal harmony and egotistical American discords. He depicted Polynesians as intensely human, their prized spontaneity, simplicity, and individuality called into doubt by burlesque laughter:

> These qualities were central to the political platform of the Whig Party of Melville's time and to the literary canon of Young America's literati, with whom Melville had increasingly close ties during the writing of *Omoo*. . . . [He had a] willingness to question the fashionable attitudes of his time and a refusal to idealize his experience. . . . His gradual withdrawal from a public writing career can be traced through the burlesque imitations in his works of those aspects of popular culture he deemed inimical to the substance and quality of life.[2]

A number of writers caught the confident, extravagant mood of American life in the two decades before the Civil War and made a living on the lecture circuit. Twain, the obvious example, turned the bawdy and euphuistic into fame and fortune. None except Melville, however, had an imagination that overleaped his own technical ineptitude and the allegorist's requirement, as Blackmur put it, "of preliminary possession of a complete and stable body of belief appropriate to the theme in hand."[3] No one has had it since. The causes of Melville's forty years of nonwriting, Blackmur said, were partly bad luck and "partly that his work discovered for itself . . . that it was not meant to be fiction. . . . [*Moby-Dick* and *Pierre*] were written out of great means of some other mode of the imagination."[4]

Novel is the only label we have for Melville's long fictions even if they are dramatically weak and even if a central character such as Ahab is not a great character but a great figure. By adapting Blackmur's definition of *form*—"Form is the way things go together in their medium"—we can understand the medium for *Moby-Dick* as a theory of art that is a philosophy of life. We do not have the romantic concept that the chaos of art mirrors the chaos of life but a humanistic skepticism according to which the bounded imagination works equally on what is inside and what is outside. The whaling ship provided Melville the verisimilitude necessary for credible romance and the external force for shaping dramatic scenes. Exaggerating the discrete figures on board often made each seem an allegorical complex of allusions shifted from classical myth to modern philosophy. For example, Ahab appears Promethean: He waves his fiery harpoon; he is fatally proud; he intends to steal the whale from the sea and to whack its head as Prometheus hit Zeus—Melville speaks of "a mighty God-like dignity inherent in the brow" of the sperm whale—and he is melancholic, consumed by his own internal vulture. Melville knew Aeschylus's play, but the Promethean reference in "The Chart" chapter comes with the reinforcement of Francis Bacon and Robert Burton: Bacon's Prometheus represented self-inflicted torment from deep thinking; Burton's, from secret grief—"Sweet grief is a cannibal of its own Heart."[5]

By adding intellectual resonance, Melville gives the figure volume. His representation of the ship creates space for the sailors and for the exigencies of life on board; his evocation of cultural tradition goes back before his own anachronistic, idiosyncratic language to a supralinguistic consciousness. There is an undefinable awareness behind the words. We seem to finger a mystery, something we know we cannot know the meaning of. A great contest remains uncompleted. Melville's raw imagination seems to have grasped for an instant the explosion of energy that began the world and that threatens to end it and to have initiated us.

Such transformation proceeds from the transformation of language, in the long view a self-modulating process. Each change of social conditions enhances or restricts the possibilities of social change; each genetic mutation effects a future organism; and each change in taste, in structure, in perception formally brings about a different art. Like experimental scientists, artistic innovators discover new sights by discovering new ways of seeing. The painter changes the experience of color by changing its use; the poet reshapes diction by augmenting the meanings of words. Although we often seek strangeness, a vision to accommodate our sense of change, in perspective the changes seem to have occurred necessarily and independently, as if European languages developed their fundamental reordering of grammar and syntax from inflected Greek and Latin to uninflected French and English all by themselves without human speakers. In practice, each serious writer takes and remakes his own language. Sometimes, the writer's own work coincides with large-scale, sociolinguistic change, as Dante's prosody shaped Italian and Rabelais's fiction helped build modern French. Such magnified examples show clearly that, as Cimabue said, art proceeds from art.

Perhaps because we suppose it is not to be applied, we expect a philosophic theory, like a mathematical proof, to be validated by the thoroughness with which it demonstrates its assumptions. Perhaps because we are tricked by the hocus-pocus of superficial imitation, we forget that a novel takes its strength even as a societal refractor from the way it extends its language. In the sense that Pound said, "No social order will make a draughtsman like Picasso," literature, like *Typee*, that samples strange and exotic landscapes is less importantly romance than a measure of the limits of the language and, therefore, of the consciousness in which it is written. Because the philosopher's assumptions, like the novelist's experience, reflect the manners and morality of his time, his arguments apply to his society. Similarly, the novelist judges what men do by weighing their actions in the scale he makes out of his language's tradition.

Ishmael called the *Pequod* his Harvard and Yale, his first serious institution for measuring himself. For Melville, the important yardsticks were Bayle's *Dictionary*, Plato's *Phaedo*, and Thomas Browne's *Religio Medici*, in the spirit of which Melville said, "I love to lose myself in a mystery, to pursue my reason to an O, Altitudo!"; also, the kit of the sea story as it expanded in the period 1820–50: Michael Scott's *The Pirate* (1822); Cooper's *The Pilot* (1823), *Afloat and Ashore* (1844), and *Miles Wallingford* (1844); and the nautical tales of Joseph Holt Ingraham, C. J. Peterson, who wrote under the pseudonym "Harry Danforth," Edward Z. C. Judson, and M. M. Ballou. The Harvard man Nathaniel Ames published *A Mariner's Sketches* in 1830; Joseph C. Hart, his fictionalized *Miriam Coffin; or, the Whale-Fisherman* in 1834. Jeremiah Reynolds's diaries of five years' whaling in the Pacific underlay his accounts of the phantasmagoric "Mocha Dick" that *Knickerbocker Magazine* published in 1839. Believing the entrance to the hollow earth was in the polar region, he sponsored the exploration written up in Charles Wilkes's lavishly illustrated six-volume *Narrative of the U.S. Exploring Expedition 1838–1842*, which Melville bought in 1847.[6]

Dana's *Two Years Before the Mast* appeared in 1840. In that year, N. P. Willis, foreign correspondent for the *New York Mirror,* published more of his European travel notes, *Letters from Under a Bridge, and Poems,* and *Loiterings of Travel.* Bayard Taylor's European sketches written for the *New York Tribune* were collected in *Views A-foot; or, Europe Seen with Knapsack and Staff* in 1846. Unpublished journals, poems, tales, and dramas—such as Samuel Braly's, George Gould's, Ambrose Bates's, B. F. Rogers's, or Orrin Smalley's not collected until 1979 by Pamela Miller in *And the Whale Is Ours*—had small or no circulation, but sometimes such accounts were passed from hand to hand on ship or between ships at a gam. When the *Acushnet* gammed with the *Lima* in midsummer 1841, Melville received from Owen Chase's son a copy of Chase's 1821 *Narrative of the Shipwreck of the Whale Ship Essex.* That Melville knew all this equipment is affirmed by quotations in his fiction and by a review he wrote for Duyckinck's *Literary World* in March 1847 of J. Ross Browne's 1846 *Etchings of a Whaling Cruise*: "Of late years there have been revealed so many plain, matter-of-fact details connected with nautical life, that, at the present day, the poetry of salt water is very much on the wane. . . . Browne's narrative tends still further to impair the charm with which poetry and fiction have invested the sea."

Most of this material was simplistic and emotional. Written to tell about remote paradises and life at sea, it celebrated earthly Edens or exposed the indecent sufferings of the sailors whose labor made the new commerce possible or did both. As Melville wrote Murray, his English publisher, about *Typee,* "The interest of the book almost wholly consists in the *intrinsick merit of the narrative alone*. . . . [It] is certainly calculated for popular reading, or for none at all. . . . However [it] must at last be believed on its own account—they believe it here now—a little touched up they say but *true*."[7] Even in *Typee* Melville changed the form of the tale by focusing on the narrator's responses; that is, he exploited the psychology of the told story, as did Dostoevsky. Especially in *Moby-Dick*, by blending blubber and poetry—by creating as a form a medium that also carried the illusion of a real story—he built an allusive schema of symbolic meaning. In a letter to Dana in May 1850, he said his recipe would yield "a strange sort of a book, tho', I fear; blubber is blubber you know; tho' you may get oil out of it, the poetry runs as hard as sap from a frozen maple tree;—& to cook the thing up, one must needs throw in a little fancy, which from the nature of the thing, must be as ungainly as the gambols of the whales themselves."[8]

Moby-Dick failed with readers because it was a formal mutation—"So much trash belonging to the worst school of Bedlam literature," the *Atheneum*'s reviewer said. A sharp and friendly intelligence like Hawthorne understood it, but for seventy-five years most readers did not suspect the horoscopic import of a sentence from *Redburn*: "Divine imaginings, like gods, come down to the groves of our Thessalies, and there, in the embrace of wild, dryad reminiscences, beget the beings that astonish the world."[9]

Dostoevsky's popularity, eclipsed by Siberian imprisonment and exile, increased with his vivid novels of the 1860s and 1870s and his antireformist, "prophetic" views offered in *A Writer's Diary* and in his speech at the Pushkin Commemoration. In his life's work, he studied the meaning of innocence—how the individual commits himself to social life through idealism and self-conceptualization, embodied in the figure of the fragile, sensitive, inquisitive, precocious child victimized by poverty and humiliation, morbidly responsive to injustice. Even in his first fiction, *Poor People,* the illusional house of life that the childlike characters inhabit was built by literary change: Makar Devushkin honors what he thinks is Pushkin's national piety and castigates what he calls Gogol's lampoons and the nonsense of Shakespeare, thereby enacting Dostoevsky's new realism, asserting in literature the realness of those who reject literature.

In 1876, in the revived *A Writer's Diary,* Dostoevsky repeated his devotion to children: "Long ago I set myself the goal of writing a novel about contemporary Russian children, and about their contemporary fathers, too, of course, in their contemporary interrelations. The epic is ready and was a thing created, above all, the way a novelist's work must always be. I take fathers and children from all social levels, insofar as possible, and follow the children from earliest childhood." The projected but never realized "The Life of a Great Sinner" had proposed such a novel in 1869–70; the first part of *The Adolescent* had achieved an aspect of it in 1875; *The Karamazov Brothers* dramatized the middle ground; but in none of the work did Dostoevsky show the extent to which his study depended on literary models. We may put it the other way round by saying that his Russianness came out in his language, for no other Slavic literature developed the cult of The Goal, the eschatological Either/Or that Alyosha and Myshkin and Stavrogin embody, and no other Slavic language so connoted "gloom, darkness and power," Milosz said; "in the language is all there is to know about Russia."[10]

During the 1875 Christmas season, Dostoevsky attended a children's party at the St. Petersburg Artists' Club, ran into a seven-year-old beggar on the street, and visited a reformatory on the city outskirts. He described his visit there with A. F. Koni in the January 1876 issue of *A Writer's Diary,* where he also referred to the artists' party and the little beggar:

> During the Christmas holidays, and on Christmas Eve, in fact, on such-and-such a street corner I several times met a young boy, no more than about seven. In the terrible cold he was dressed practically in summer clothes, his neck wrapped in an old rag, which did show that somebody had gotten him ready, sending him out. He had his "hand out," a term meaning that he was begging. These little boys made the term up themselves. There are many like him. They swarm in front of you and wail what they have memorized. But this one did not wail and spoke, I thought, innocently and strangely and stared in my face trustingly, showing that he was probably just beginning his profession. To my questions he replied that his sister was out of work, sick. Perhaps it was true, but I later learned that there are hordes of these little boys, sent forth with their "hands out," even in the most awful cold, and if they do not get anything, they probably have a beating coming.

The same issue of the *Diary* included "The Boy at Christ's Christmas Party" after the report of the actual beggar, a report that began, "Children are a strange people; they dream and have visions."

In Dostoevsky's notebooks, the entry for December 30, 1875, reads: "Christmas party. The child in Rückert. Christ, ask Vladimir Rafailovich Zotov." Friedrich Rückert, a German romantic poet known for translations of Eastern poetry, was popular in Russia in the 1840s in Zhukovsky's versions. In 1861, Zotov's magazine *Illustration* ran a piece on Rückert.[11] An 1816 poem of Rückert's attracted Dostoevsky—a sentimental, moralistic ballad entitled "A Solitary Child's Christmas," often reprinted in German anthologies of children's verse but never translated into Russian. Dostoevsky may have first heard about it from his brother, a Germanist, or learned of it during his stay in

Germany, or come on a reference to it during that 1875 holiday season and turned to Zotov for the original or to ask about translation. Consisting of eighteen five-line stanzas, the poem reads in part:

Es läuft ein fremdes Kind
Am Abend vor Weihnachten
Durch eine Stadt geschwind,
Die Lichter zu betrachten,
Die angezündet sind.

Es steht vor jedem Haus
Und sieht die hellen Räume,
Die drinnen schaun heraus,
Die lampenvollen Bäume;
Weh wird's ihm überaus.

. . . .

Da kommt mit einem Licht
Durch's Gässlein hergewallet,
Im weissen Kleide schlicht,
Ein ander Kind;—wie schallet
Es lieblich, da es spricht:

"Ich bin der heil'ge Christ,
War auch ein Kind vordessen,
Wie du ein Kindlein bist.
Ich will dich nicht vergessen,
Wenn alles dich vergisst; . . ."

. . . .

Es ward ihm wie ein traum;
Da langten hergebogen
Englein herab vom Baum
Zum Kindlein, das sie zogen
Hinauf zum lichten Raum.

A solitary child
In the dusk of Christmas Eve
Runs through the city streets,
Staring at the lights,
Entranced by all it sees.

It halts at every house
To peer at lighted rooms
In light that's pouring out,
At candle-brightened trees;
And heavy grows its heart.

. . . .

Then with a light there comes
Another child across
The street, dressed all in white,
Whose voice is marvelous
And who says with love:

"I am the Holy Christ,
Who also was a child,
A little child like you.
I won't forget you ever,
When all the others do; . . ."

. . . .

The child thought this a dream;
But then little angels came
Down from the tree to the child
And took it away with them
Up to the Room of Light.

Das fremde Kindlein ist	The solitary child
Zur Heimat nun gekehret,	Is now at home at last,
Bei seinem heil'gen Christ;	Now with its Holy Christ;
Und was hier wird bescheeret,	And what would happen here
Es dorten leicht vergisst.[12]	It will readily forget.

Rückert's narrative is conventionalized. Dostoevsky's story contrasts city and country, makes the child a boy and, leaning on the physiological writers and on Gogol's phantasmagoric "Nevsky Prospect," animates city life. Rückert's child is cold and lonely, but Dostoevsky's little boy is cold, lonely, poor, and terrified and feels himself center stage. The parents of Rückert's child are too busy to pay attention. Loved by his mother, Dostoevsky's child is a victim of the war between the rich and the poor in which his mother is helpless. Unlike Rückert's child, who goes alone, Dostoevsky's boy reaches Christ with a crowd of "his own." Rückert moralizes; his child first confronts Christ on the street, then experiences a dreamy feeling. Dostoevsky dramatizes; his boy freezes to death and, dying and in death, envisions Christ in the flesh, combining the actual and the fantastic. His pain is not alienable. The story carries a political message, certainly, but even stronger is the dramatization of suffering to which there is neither end nor answer.

Ironically, most French and American intellectuals who turned to Dostoevsky after World War II, thinking him a precursor of existentialism, admired him for nonliterary reasons. Tastes keep changing, however, and so do values. After the atrocities of that war, man may have seemed not only forked and naked but also unredeemably degenerate. On the other hand, a writer's distancing himself from his own faith, as Gide did, allows him disinterestedly to contemplate the world as it is, including Auerbach's *figurae* individually and in their patterns, and to express a political understanding, no matter how irrelevant, and an abiding love of sensual beauty and energy. Craft is not precious refinement; craft lies in making durable a fragile, often inconsistent but humanly truthful vision. Its subject may be gross and violent—killing two old women with an axe, or boiling down blubber—but the creative work, Blok said, is all delicate flowers, and we must not lean our elbows on it.[13]

5
Modes

> To search, to adapt to his own art and time what others have discovered, to make *experiments*—that is one of the poet's most important tasks.
>
> —*Bryusov*

WHETHER AN AUTHOR INVENTS HIS FICtional figures—liberates them from objective conditions by his imagination—or whether the figures by their objective nature imprison the author—oblige him to fulfill the design of his creative work—we habitually dislike an autobiographical figure that violates the pattern of a narrated life, and we are depressed by samples of detached imagination. At most, we are now amused by Villiers de l'Isle-Adam's exaggeratedly sensitive Axël, who tells his lover Sara that the earth is an illusion and that to live would be sacrilege against their souls. "As for living, our servants will do that for us," he says. And we agree with Lermontov that we do not like to be set up. Introducing Pechorin's diary in *A Hero of Our Time,* he said, "The trouble with Rousseau's *Confessions* is that he read it to his friends." A work of fiction must be true to life, we say without specifying what life and without knowing how to define *true.* Life has something to do with objectivity; truth has something to do with interpretation. The better our taste, the more we believe that we are able simultaneously to weigh the merits of the dispute between Auden's poet "encased in talent like a uniform" and the figure fixed in prose by the laws of the material. We say that the struggle itself is what matters. We refuse to judge *Redburn* on

Melville's assurance to Dana that it was written "almost entirely for 'lucre'—by the job, as a woodsawyer saws wood."[1] Money is a motive for a man's actions; it is not a quality of the actions themselves. We will not judge *Typee* on Melville's assertion of his "anxious desire to speak the unvarnished truth,"[2] for Melville himself said that he never had evidence that the Typees were cannibals.

Mode is contentious. The means that disengages a figure engages an author. And the other way round. In the preface to his unfinished novel "The Pearl of Creation," Chernyshevsky spoke of his desire

> to write a purely objective novel in which there would not be a trace of my own attitudes and of my personal sympathies. . . . I think that for me, a man of strong and firm convictions, hardest of all would be writing like Shakespeare: He describes people and life without showing what he himself thinks about the problems his characters must solve as best they can. Othello says "Yes," Iago says "No"—Shakespeare says nothing. . . . Apply the first line of the epigraph to my novel—
>
> *Wie Schnee, so weiss,*
> *Und kalt, wie Eis—*
>
> and the second, to me.[3]

His objectivity is, of course, specious. However much he wished to create a new means of disengagement, he was actually establishing a bias. A novel without love interest? With no indication of how the author takes himself? Even if instructional, such a schema would not lead to objectivity.

Rather, objectivity depends on the mode of narration. Bakhtin says that in Dostoevsky's work it is created by his polyphonic structure destroying the old monologic (that is, romantic) novel by introducing the author as a figure in debate with each of the characters, a consciousness "that reflects and conjures up in its mind not a world of objects but specifically these other consciousnesses with their own worlds, reconstitutes them in their actual inconclusiveness (in precisely that lies their essence)."[4] Literary objectivity is not the sum of characteristics of a mutable, physical world, which we sometimes influence by will and to which we ourselves sometimes bend in understanding of necessity. It is the manipulation of eternal partiality, the keeping the debate going.

The narrator is master of ceremonies. Frequently, Dostoevsky makes him an inoffensive, undefined reporter informed of everything, with a photographic memory, who, by reenacting the ordering of events in his consciousness, serves as a prism between the events in the book and their completion in the reader's mind. The narrator has no characterizing personality. In dialogue, he is the straight man. Insofar as the debate among the actors weaves a pattern of consciousness, he has no amour propre. Through his consciousness we see the partiality of each actor's claim and the impartiality of the achieved pattern. By rubbing the actors together, the narrator sets each limited claim in the wider context that he is recording without refuting the legitimacy of any claim and without reflecting the truthfulness of the content of each self-consciousness. What is adequate to each man is finally given in confession, such as Stavrogin's deleted from *The Demons,* but its adequacy to the pattern is affirmed through the narrator who, for the sake of impersonal consciousness, does not allow one excessive claim to disfigure the design. Dostoevsky prefaces "A Gentle Soul" with an author's note that reads in part:

> Now about the story itself. I have subtitled it "fantastic," even though I myself consider it supremely real. But the fantastic is in this instance actual, in the form of the story itself. . . .

Slowly [the husband] *explains* the thing to himself and "pulls his thoughts together." A series of memories irresistibly brings him at last to the *truth*; the truth irresistibly ennobles his mind and heart. Toward the end, even the tone of the story changes, compared to its disorderly beginning. . . .

If a stenographer could have overheard him and written everything down, it would have come out rougher, more unfinished, than I have it, but, as far as I can see, the psychological pattern would likely be the same. You would make the assumption that a stenographer wrote it all down, after which I supposedly finished it in written form, and that is what I call the fantastic in this story. Something like this has often occurred in art: Victor Hugo, for example, in his chef-d'oeuvre *Le dernier jour d'un condamné* used almost the exact same device and, though he did not introduce a stenographer, achieved even greater verisimilitude by assuming that a condemned man can (and has the time to) write down notes not only on his last day but even in his last hour and literally at the last moment. If he had not entertained this fantasy, the work itself would never have existed—the most real and most truthful thing of all he ever wrote.[5]

Other authors are narrators who take the reader on a tour. Like Tolstoy, they compose the reader into their patterns. As Bakhtin said, "Tolstoy's monolithic, naïve point of view and his judgments penetrate everywhere, . . . subordinating everything to their single-minded unity."[6]

Melville's narrators do not control the symbolism, the meaning of which is built up by the story each tells. Even the irony of which they are capable, directed always to the "actual situation" in the narrative, does not exceed it. In "Bartleby, the Scrivener" or in *Moby-Dick,* the narrator's consciousness and the author's are separate if only in the temporal sense that one precedes the other. Ishmael begins by identifying himself and detailing his excuse for having been there. Then, like Tolstoy, he takes us on a tour:

Circumambulate the city of a dreamy Sabbath afternoon. Go from Corlears Hook to Coenties Slip, and from thence, by Whitehall, northward. What do you see?—Posted like silent sentinels all around the town, stand thousands upon thousands of mortal men fixed in ocean reveries. Some leaning against the spiles; some seated upon the pier-heads; some looking over the bulwarks of ships from China; some high aloft in the rigging, as if striving to get a still better seaward peep. But these are all landsmen; of week days pent up in lath and plaster—tied to counters, nailed to benches, clinched to desks. How then is this? Are the green fields gone? What do they here?

But look! here come more crowds, pacing straight for the water, and seemingly bound for a dive.[7]

A superior guide, energetic and experienced, the narrator is an intermediary between the external world of desert and sea and our human attitudes to it. He does not portray himself, but he does not efface himself, either. His enthusiasm, his disinterestedness, and his intelligence interpret the world's images from an outsider's point of view, as in chapter 27 of *Moby-Dick*: "Long usage had, for this Stubb, converted the jaws of death into an easy chair. What he thought of death itself, there is no telling." Ishmael cites "facts" and chronicles "events," includes the specifics of cetology and spins out allegorical meanings of the whiteness of the whale. He stands as an eternal witness, physical and spiritual like Turgenev's "born observer," who sees everything but has no self-will. He is young, freeborn, pensive, inquisitive. Others are not, but even if a Melville narrator is a mellowed old hearty who combines "tolerance, whimsy, acceptance of things-as-they-are [with] genial heartiness and humor of response,"[8] he remains uncommitted and uncompromised, sympathetic to the goodness of "The Divine Inert"[9] and able to report on the willful passion of an Ahab "with a crucifixion in his face; in all the nameless regal overbearing dignity of some mighty woe."[10]

Writing on Balzac, Ramon Fernandez identified the dramatic mode with the novel (*roman*) and the narrative mode with the yarn (*récit*): "The novel is a representation of events that take place in time, a representation including the conditions of those events' appearance and development. The yarn is a presentation of events that have taken place the reproduction of which is regulated by a narrator in conformity with rules of exposition and persuasion. . . . The novel is a spontaneously and immediately evocative work. On the one hand, the yarn observes rational sequentiality and the intellectual laws of combination; on the other, painting and the general laws of description."[11] Like most critics, he called the dramatic mode better.

Berthoff defended Melville and the narrative mode, saying that the told story had predominated in the United States because of America's unsettled social order, the "underlying monotony of personal existence," and authors' desires to "capture household and regional vernaculars."[12]

Both modes have long existed side by side everywhere. Leskov's "The Left-hander" and Lardner's "Haircut" are famous examples from different centuries of suspenseful, manipulated, told stories. They remind us that an author does not choose his fictional mode. It is forced on him by tradition, by training, by the obduracy of his material, and by the "logic" of his design. It must combine the immediacy of experience and the permanency of meaning, the concrete event and the thought arising from it.

Dostoevsky's debaters, like Raskolnikov, argue with such intense and equal partiality that they turn ideas into events.

Melville's adventurer retails a series of events in such a way that we discover their price in ideas.

Dostoevsky sets his characters in a ring around a central, threatening problem and then makes them exchange positions in elaborate dance, bringing the outside in and the inside out.

Melville sets up parallels between men and aspirations, between events and meaning, combining the two by intervention of the author's disinterested, often ironic intelligence. As he wrote in *Moby-Dick,* "Out of the trunk, the branches grow; out of them, the twigs. So, in productive subjects, grow the chapters."[13]

The New York crowds at Coenties Slip seem "bound for a dive"; the great whale dives; Ishmael dives "as a ghost" after he has made his fourth will; but apart from all, underlying all, is Melville's consciousness pushing against his characters and beyond his narrator, as he indicated in a letter to Duyckinck: "I love all men who *dive*. . . . the whole corps of thought-divers, that have been diving & coming up again with blood-shot eyes since the world began."[14]

Rubbed against each other, Dostoevsky's characters work against themselves, resolving nothing, labeling everything, until the composition is perfect and we cannot separate one mode from another. Lost in our dive, we are ready to rebegin in our minds, as the Man in the Cellar says, "A novel must have a hero, but here *deliberately* brought together are all the characteristics for an anti-hero. . . . We're stillborn, and for a long time haven't come from living fathers, and we like it more and more. We're acquiring a taste for it. Soon we'll invent getting born from an idea."[15]

6
To Tell the Truth

> There is no more place for a privileged observer in a real novel than in the world of Einstein. . . . In the eyes of God, Who cuts through appearances and goes beyond them, there is no novel, no art, for art thrives on appearances. God is not an artist.
>
> —*Sartre*

THROUGH YOUNG DEDALUS'S DECLARATION to forge in the smithy of his soul the uncreated conscience of his race, Joyce flaunted the bootlessness masked by modernism, the state of incommensurability called the Absurd. Social formlessness has overcome the aesthetic strictness of conventional figuration, naturalistic style, and sentimental plotting, but postmodern writers have not construed a new moral form. Scientifically and philosophically speaking, if anything can properly be said to exist there must be acceptable conditions of, and criteria for, identification and individuation. Created conscience, like the existence of a god or whatever conscience depends on, is an idea conceivable only with certain emotions characteristic of the conceptual act, a leap of faith willed in full consciousness beyond the otherwise untransgressible limit of philosophy. As Dostoevsky dramatized, wanting to believe is a necessary condition for believing. Belief, however, as Socrates explained to Glaucon in *The Republic,* is one of the "many conventional notions of the mass of mankind, adrift in a sort of twilight between pure reality and pure unreality," neither refutable nor verifiable, and the will to believe may lead to nothing significant. The smaller we see ourselves to be, the more remote or more arbitrary our gods until we cannot shrink further and the gods are out of sight. From a modern, philosophic point of view, nothing we attribute to our gods is meaningful; in fact, as Ayer points out, it is not clear by what criteria such spiritual substances as gods or souls can be said to exist. Ordinarily, when asked what we are talking about, we produce the object or list its properties, but among spiritual substances what is it that has the properties? Locke's "something we know not what."[1] The old rituals of fortune-telling, games of chance, and prayer that once aligned a community with its deities are now private, desperate acts beseeching favor in an indifferent world. And the man who would tell the truth, the whole truth, and nothing but the truth finds himself in the condition of the philosopher Cratylus who, having resolved never to make a statement that he was not certain was true, ended up wagging his finger.

Despite their religious convictions and their idiosyncratic philosophies, Dostoevsky and Melville are turned into existentialists. In contemporary jargon, the popular view is that "*Moby Dick*, as no other work of our times, presents the basic situation within which the problematic of modern man develops: the 'death of God' and the alienation of man. . . . The situation from which both Dostoievsky's rebels and his exiles start and which they try either to escape or to affirm is that of the alienation of modern man."[2] A sort of theological conspiracy encourages the misunderstanding: "Existential mistrust . . . is the destruction of confidence in existence. . . . At its core the conflict between mistrust and trust of man conceals the conflict between the mistrust and trust of eternity."[3]

Neither Dostoevsky nor Melville was a philosopher, much less a logical positivist. Both assumed that man was spiritually real—that the soul exists—and that events had multiple causes—that for any event there are several reference systems of explanation no one of which is adequate. Repeatedly, both indirectly asked one question: Assuming that divine love bore and binds the universe, and given the antagonism between belief and unbelief and the difficulties of presenting an artistic picture of the nature of love, can an artistic picture be sufficient response to the philosophic issues?

For years the scientific habit of mind assumed an endlessly interconnected physical world existing according to descriptive laws and independent of any observer. So apt did this assumption seem that Pavlov applied it under laboratory conditions to neurological states, successfully demonstrating the physical interconnectedness of sound and neural reflex. Every event in space and time could be measured; what could not be measured did not have meaning.

Einstein's theory of relativity and a number of associated concepts, such as Heisenberg's uncertainty principle, remind us forcefully that what we call space and time do not exist independently of our observations. They are aspects of our apprehension of events in what, because we otherwise cannot even conceive it, we call space-time. They are the basic modes of our consciousness; without them, nothing occurs to us. Mathematical space-time, the most useful of them, allows us to do a good deal of work toward establishing an understanding of universal energy, but of course, we also understand that we cannot think outside the categories with which we think. Only a metaphor maker can escape the limitations of usual space and time.

Space and time are not substances or substantial properties. Space-time is an intellectual projection on an otherwise immeasurable universe. Laboratory experiment is no longer regarded as verifying causality or proving truth; it is seen to corroborate clever but always limited hypotheses. Which comes first: the assumptions and axioms, or the verbal and mathematical ways of thinking that seem to depend on them? I suspect that first comes cast of mind, like our innate capacity for grammatical arrangement, and that over a lifetime it adjusts assumptions to experience. Strong minds—reasoning minds and metaphorizing minds alike—do not strive for immortality but seek to overcome restrictions in their own categories of thinking. Tolstoy's remark that any thinking man is always thinking about his own death does not say that he is afraid to die but, rephrasing Montaigne, that he is trying to outthink his limitations. A strong mind struggles to reach into the next dimension, even at its own expense, as we find in *Billy Budd* and *The Idiot.*

In the naturalist or classical realist conventions, Budd and Myshkin appear as defective figures, men unable at critical moments to express themselves adequately to others. Both are tagged in order to be associated allegorically with figures outside literary convention, "Angel Billy" and "Prince Christ." In the cause-and-effect world of common sense and workaday life, where justice is arbitrated by men, both lose appropriately, and the tags point to a source of a different judgment. If we consider as dominant neither the details and requirements of verisimilitude nor the import of allegory but the "argument," or proposals, of the fiction, then each protagonist is seen trying to reform the social conventions around him by reaching beyond his own adequacy. The classical literary mode to express winning is comedy; to express losing, tragedy. The modes themselves have been reformed since the disappearance of the Olympian aristocracy and the loss of the sense of greatness.

The more man has transformed nature and the longer he has lived with internalized values, expecting happiness finally not in this world but in the next, the more aggressive he has become, and the more difficult for him to measure his relation to space and time. Long a metaphor to house a moral judgment, "apocalypse" is now literally predictable: Man can do it himself. Neither Melville nor Dostoevsky could expect such practical destruction as we do. They could not believe that misery was perverted greatness, as did Sophocles, or that dialectics could be politically useful, as did Plato. Their heroes had to be extraordinary men in ordinary clothing, and they themselves—Dostoevsky, the stenographer's husband, and Melville, the judge's son-in-law—like Flaubert's ideal writer had "to think like a demigod" but "to live like a bourgeois."

In nineteenth-century industrial society, there was no aristocracy of tragedy, no appeal to the goodness of common reason. Concepts of justice had to come from beyond the limits of nationalism, Protestantism, and cartels. The only widely believed mythic stuff lay in the Bible, and the biblical view of misery is not tragic but ironic, as Northrop Frye noted.[4] The Book of Job sharply differentiates between winning and losing, but the mind cannot reason the difference. The transformations of nature are God's work, too grand for human comprehension. By the middle of the nineteenth century, however, nothing seemed too grand for the captains of industry to master save man's soul itself, into whose darknesses both Dostoevsky and Melville drove their heroes. For having tried to make intelligible a pattern of energy he could not articulate the terms of, Budd was hanged and Myshkin was reduced to idiocy.

Quixote's ridiculous naïveté enhances his goodness. His chivalric ideals cover, then reveal, monarchism, colonialism, mercantilism, capitalism, but in the happy valley of the imagination where he begins and we end the book, we share his absurdity and support his morality. We prefer things his way, even though and because they are not. Budd and Myshkin are ridiculous not because they have chosen to pickle their minds in old books but because society does not know how to include them and their self-knowledge, and they cannot find a way.

There are many stories of *Jesus redivivus,* the miraculous reappearance of the historic Jesus in a subsequent time. Modern versions, beside Lawrence's *The Man Who Died,* include *The Magic Mountain,* in which Chauchat bounces in with Peeperkorn for "The Last Supper," and *The Master and Margarita,* in which sad-faced, almost pathological Ivan Nikolayich tells his story and plays his role of savior as mad outcast. According to Theodore Ziolkowski, Dostoevsky, like Nietzsche, exploited the ancient association of "divine truth with madness: in the eyes of society the savior or redeemer appears as a fool."[5] This opinion assumes the canons of literary naturalism, the dogma of a dualistic world in which only discursive, or "scientific," or historical explanation is correct. According to it, a story may be appealing or morally instructive but not true. For example, Ziolkowski says that to make Myshkin "plausible as a human being,

Dostoevsky found it necessary to mar his moral beauty with certain flaws."[6] That his epilepsy should be considered a "flaw" rather than an aspect of his limited, human condition, like Oedipus's clubfoot, shows how bifurcated and nontragic our thinking has become.

A similar sense of smallness is expressed in Milton Stern's judgment of Billy Budd's death as a "sacrifice of self to the historical moment,"[7] and in Martin Pops's declaration "that Melville's formulation of the dualistic cosmos, the worlds of the Secular and Sacred, derives ultimately from the primitive quest for the Center and from the symbolism of sexuality."[8] In Melville's work, the secular is frequently presented sexually and the sacred is represented by silence, just as Billy Budd and Pierre Glendinning are two of Melville's Christ figures whose sacrifices are allegorically conspicuous and more or less inevitable, given the juridical, economic, sexual, and political limitations of the systems they serve. A bit of bad luck sets Billy on his downward (or upward) course, a gesture hardly less accidental than Philoctetes' wandering into the god's shrine, for which he suffered poisonous snakebite—or Tommo's leg infection in *Typee.* Sophocles is interested in how the hero takes his agony and how he takes himself; Melville wants to know what it means. Whatever his own suffering was, whatever he understood, Sophocles assumed that man's world was the only real one. Disillusioned, Melville, like Dostoevsky, could not accept that.

In his copy of Schopenhauer's *Studies in Pessimism,* Melville marked the following passage: "The sole thing that reconciles me to the Old Testament is the story of the Fall. In my eyes, it is the only metaphysical truth in that book, even though it appears in the form of an allegory."[9] Every fiction that exemplifies truth leads to an incomprehensible combustion. The story does not burn, saved by its proportions and properties, but some heroic figure or some mind is mysteriously driven beyond itself by the conflict between its own energy and its own inadequacy. Even more Christ-like than Myshkin or Budd is the humble, proud, almost speechless Bartleby, whom Melville meant, says D. M. Fiene, "to be an incarnation of Christ. . . . Melville deliberately set out to dramatize the confrontation of a Christian with the Messiah, Christ Returned, at the time of the Apocalypse. With a fine sense of irony, Melville has depicted the Messiah not as the glorious Son descending in a cloud with all his holy angels, but as the least of Christ's brethren."[10]

Day by day, the epileptic is a misfit and the drudge is unremarkable. The mighty of this world care little for them. In my reading, neither Dostoevsky nor Melville dignifies such lives by artificially implanting spirit, by turning those people into movable religious property. Is Hans Prager right? Is Dostoevsky repeating "the attempt of Plato and Kant" to bring the "kingdom of . . . immediate actuality . . . into indissoluble connection with that of spirit, the invisible ultimate basis of the world of experience?"[11] By emphasizing one issue or another of the cultural traditions in which they wrote, you can make Melville a classicist or a Calvinist; Dostoevsky, a philosopher or a faithful Eastern Christian. Golosovker set *The Karamazov Brothers* alongside *The Critique of Pure Reason* and found four sets of antitheses in Dostoevsky's work:

1. Is the universe created and finite?
   (or: Infinite and endless?)

2. Is there immortality?
   (or: Is everything destructible?)
3. Has man free will?
   (or: Is there only natural necessity?)
4. Does God exist, creator of the universe?
   (or: Is there no god?)

These parallel four sets of dogmatic-antinomic categories in Kant's work:

1. The world began in time and is bound in space.
   (or: The world has no beginning in time or space; it is endless)
2. Every complex substance consists of simple parts; there exist only simple substance and what it composes.
   (or: No complex thing exists of simple parts; in general, no simple substance exists)
3. Causality, according to physical laws, does not explain all phenomena; one must also suppose free will.
   (or: There is no freedom; everything occurs according to physical laws)
4. Some inevitable Being is attached to the universe, either as part or as cause.
   (or: There is absolutely no necessary Being either within or without the universe that is its cause)[12]

Golosovker maintains that Kant's categories, which experience can neither affirm nor deny and which "reason is powerless to abandon," stimulated Dostoevsky's dialectic: Dostoevsky "challenged Kant-the-Antithetical to a duel and did not hesitate to use all his weapons: sarcasm, rhetoric, blandishment, dialectical casuistry, creating by this contest the ingenious tragedies and farces that comprise the novel's chapters."[13] Golosovker's perceptive reading does not try to translate articles of faith into good works. He sees the untenability of either set of terms from the frame of the other and separates narrative movement from narrative meaning, that sense we have of what a story comes to after we have read it all.

Neither Dostoevsky nor Melville is an ironist in our contemporary way, for both believed in absolute truth and the mercy of God. Rather, they took an ironic stance toward the misery they uncovered everywhere in urban life and, vaticinal and romantic like their biblical heroes, revealed brief visions of beauty at the end of jeremiads or concealed hope itself in the tensions and sufferings of ordinary, undefinable lives. The lives are there for all to see, even untouched by the vision. Whether or not there are converts, the vision is true. The literal part of the metaphor is verified not by a spiritual basis but by common experience. The figurative part is verified by the literary dialectic that houses it and by our general acknowledgment of the myths on which it leans. The efforts to move discursively with time (narrative) and to move metaphorically backward and out of time (poetry) come together in fiction that is especially intelligible because, both serious and self-mocking, it deals with opposites on their own grounds. As reconciliation of the irreconcilable is false thinking, so the "Legend of the Grand Inquisitor" is presented as a poem.

In 1851, Melville wrote in a letter to Hawthorne that "Truth is the silliest thing under the sun. Try to get a living by the Truth—and go to the Soup Societies. . . . To the world at large are not reformers almost universally laughing-stocks? Why so? Truth is ridiculous to men."[14] A few years later, in 1868, Dostoevsky wrote to Ivanova that the evocation of sympathy was the secret of humor but that the contrast was both effective and profound: "Of the beautiful figures in Christian literature the most perfected is Don Quixote. But he is beautiful only because he is, at the same time, ridiculous."[15]

7
The Rectifying Mirror

> Laughter . . . is gaiety itself. But the philosopher who gathers a handful to taste may find that the substance is scanty, and the aftertaste bitter.
>
> —*Bergson*

THE CLOWN'S DISTORTION, LIKE THE CONFIDENCE man's masquerade, entertains us three or four times over: We like the surface play of light and wit, the rhythm and structure of his movements, both the flattery and the indictments and, finally, what he says about human nature. His duplicity is artistry. Sometimes, persuaded by a strong performance or a subtle line, we forget that there are more colors in nature than a painter can match, more sounds in the air than a composer can mix, that the power of art depends not on the accuracy of illusion so much as on its strength. The writers of the 1840s who documented city miseries showed a moral fidelity comparable to the visual fidelity of eighteenth-century French still-life painters. Their strength derived from the discrepancy between the generative, or metaphoric, power of their structure and the illustrational details with which they made their stories believable and their characters seem to be living people. Less concealed in their work—more concealed in writers of greater skill—depending on attitude, fashion, and material—this literary dialectic was a conscious self-manufacturing that made a distortion self-supporting and, therefore, true. Reading Homer aloud, we are scarcely aware that he composed his poems as he sang them, and we are so involved in the theology, cosmology, and morality of *The Divine Comedy* that we do not notice that Dante walked through the middle of it.

Melville's stories foreshorten time for structural purposes and conscious effect, as in "The Paradise of Bachelors": "The genuine Templar is long since departed. . . . [Now] the helmet is a wig. . . . The Templar is to-day a Lawyer." Like the apple, the Templar is better for having fallen: "Best of comrades, most affable of hosts, capital diner is the modern Templar. His wit and wine are both of sparkling brands."

"The Paradise of Bachelors" exposes the hypocrisy of a life dependent on one-sided advocacy. Melville pluralistically argues for anarchic self-creation. Praising things for being not more than they are, he systematically subverts hand-me-down truths in the name of responsiveness. Like Lear's Fool, he distorts in order to reassert reason. Like a clown, he mimics in order to rationalize manner. Narratively weak and histrionically tame, his short fictions express his talent for verbal drama in which he hypostatizes the extremes of a conceit and plays them like a fish on a line—wild forces brought to the surface by delicate persistence.

The impulse behind even family issues and sexual preferences that find their ways into Melville's stories lies in an attitudinal incompatibility. When Melville was born, New York's population was about 130,000; when he died, about 3 million; but all his life he looked still farther back to a semi-imaginary "olden time," as he labeled a drawing of "Arrowhead," his house in Pittsfield, sketched while sailing to San Francisco.[1] Faddish spirit rappings and frequent train wrecks provoked his objections, but his deeper thoughts were impelled by mysterious ironies. For twenty years after the Civil War, he was a customs inspector stationed at Gansevoort

Street, named, he knew, for his Revolutionary War ancestor. One May day in 1870 he stopped at the Gansevoort Hotel and asked if Gansevoort was some man's name. "Sir," an old man replied, "this hotel and the street of the same name are called after a very rich family who in old times owned a great deal of property hereabouts." Melville contrasted himself to his grandfather, who had achieved fame one hundred years earlier defending Fort Stanwix. "Repairing to the philosophic privacy of the District Office," he continued in his letter to his mother, "I then moralized upon the instability of human glory and the evanescence of—many other things."[2]

Written in the late 1880s and partly provoked by cousin Guert Gansevoort's service as first lieutenant presiding at Philip Spencer's court martial on the *Somers* in 1842, *Billy Budd* derives from Melville's sense of the irreconcilability of truth and justice. Set on opposing sides, compelled to act in one space-time, his characters put forth contrary claims and destroy each other. Like it, most of Melville's fictions are studies in values—sometimes literally black against white, as in "Benito Cereno." Suasiveness of allegory and urgency of tone dominate. Like Dostoevsky, whose narratives of intricate plot and detective fable are dominated by dramatic confrontations of ideas, Melville took special pleasure in the meaning of the manner of the telling. Not a first-rate versifier, he was a great poet of moral ambiguity.

In *Typee* the first vision of paradise contains its own contradiction. The figures of Adam and Eve are "a boy and girl, slender and graceful, and completely naked with the exception of a slight girdle of bark, from which depended at opposite points two of the russet leaves of the breadfruit tree. An arm of the boy, half screened from sight by her wild tresses, was thrown about the neck of the girl, while with the other he held one of her hands in his; and thus they stood together, their heads inclined forward, catching the faint noise we made in our progress, and with one foot in advance, as if half inclined to fly from our presence."[3] According to the Book of Genesis, man lost paradise because he transgressed. Henceforth, he had to carry a spiritual kernel within a material shell. Eden became an image of remote, inaccessible, nonintellectual happiness. But in *Typee,* Eden is defective. Although there are no snakes, man suffers the symptoms of snakebite, and although he enjoys the fruits of his quest, the fruit is rotten: "We descried a number of the trees the native name of which is 'annuee,' and which bear a most delicious fruit. . . . He quickly cleared one of the trees on which there were two or three of the fruit, but to our chagrin they proved to be much decayed; the rinds partly opened by the birds, and their hearts half-devoured. However, we quickly dispatched them, and no ambrosia could have been more delicious."[4]

Melville's praise of natural man and his ranting against the missionaries' hypocrisy suggest an iconoclastic dualism, but each experience is measured by relative standards. An event is inseparable from the terms in which it is perceived. No social system is thoroughly adequate, and no system of measurement is complete. Tommo, the narrator of *Typee*, does not want to be tattooed; intellectually he appreciates that "the whole system of tattooing was . . . connected with their religion";[5] but he also sees tattooing as a kind of clowning, an expression of the Absurd. Several years later in the narrative, when he revisits Nukuheva, he finds the king pretentiously dolled up in French military costume, "a broad patch of tattooing stretched completely across his face, in a line with his eyes, making him look as if he wore a huge pair of goggles; and royalty in goggles suggested some ludicrous ideas."[6]

The queen of Nukuheva offers even greater incongruity, for beneath her scarlet gown trimmed in yellow silk, her bare, tattooed legs resemble "two miniature Trajan's columns." At the top of the gangway, she notices "an old *salt,* whose bare arms and feet and exposed breast were covered with as many inscriptions in india ink as the lid of an Egyptian sarcophagus," and pauses. The escorting French officers try to preserve decorum, but the queen opens the sailor's shirt and lifts his trousers to see more. Then, "eager to display the hieroglyphics of her own sweet form, [she] bent forward for a moment, and turning sharply round, threw up the skirts of her mantle."[7] Carefully prepared in the conventions of comic prose, the vaudeville of the queen's tattooed ass is a histrionic joke, or mimicry, of the sort that ties *Typee* together structurally.

Melville linked separate works the same way, using a later to mock an earlier. In chapter 9 of *Pierre,* his seventh novel, he declared that "love is both Creator's and Savior's gospel to mankind; a volume bound in rose-leaves, clasped with violets, and by the beaks of humming-birds printed with peach-juice on the leaves of lilies." He was "engaging not merely in the parody of popular fiction," Martin Pops has pointed out,[8] "but in the cruelest sort of self-parody as well," parodying one of his "Fragments from a Writing Desk," his first fiction published when he was nineteen: "I picked up an elegant little, rose-colored, lavender-scented billet-doux, and hurriedly breaking the seal (a heart, transfixed with an arrow) I read by the light of the moon."

By projecting what is inexplicable and giving us a way to understand what the actors cannot, the comic gesture points back to what it overcomes—that life is materialistic, accidental, and incomprehensible. Among the Typees, its mysterious essence is represented by *taboo* guiding and controlling every action: "Anything opposed to the ordinary customs of the islanders, although not expressly prohibited, is said to be 'taboo.' "[9] Tommo, the questing stranger, is taboo. Marnoo, the alien messenger, is taboo. Neither belongs in "The Happy Valley." The balance between "in" and "out" is unstable, desires change; man constantly loses his equilibrium. The most serious failures are failures of instinct, from which follow fear and lack of self-control. The ship that Tommo quit because the captain had not kept its covenants becomes "ship," a concept, an end in itself, and ironically the means of escape from the paradise to which he had previously fled.

"Happiness is the End at which all things aim," Aristotle said and lectured that within the action of dramatic presentation there must be nothing irrational. In *Typee*, the psychologically irrational become shaping motives: Tommo's fear of the Typees, his mysteriously reswollen leg, and his lack of control over his life bring the idyll to an end. He, who after six months' whaling longed to see a blade of grass, after four months in lush Eden longs for the "glorious sight and sound of ocean." You can laud his quest or charge him with fancying that the grass is always greener on the other side, but neither response is fair. Step after step, he has been thwarted, if not taunted, by the world's self-mockery. People do things that cannot be clowned into sense. His love affair with gentle, exquisite, inarticulate Fayaway ends in sexual redundancy, she clinging to him to the last, he tossing her a bolt of cotton cloth as the boat pulls off and leaves her weeping on the shore. Abstractly, too, there is no physical paradise, for the "ship," man's ideal portable home and microcosmic society, the bright vessel of his quest, turns into a joke when sailed too far. The process of actualizing an ideal perverts it.

The old whaler *The Perseverance* is "somewhere in the vicinity of the ends of the earth." Her ancient crew of twenty is scarcely fit for Greenwich pensions or Snug Harbor; the halyards and sheets are reeved through snatch blocks and run off the windlass; the hull is caked with barnacles; and three sharks (not angels) follow like pets. Delicate, heterosexual love with Fayaway came to a tear-jerking end; the homosexual brotherhood of sailors ends in self-mockery: *The Perseverance* "never reached home, and I suppose she is still regularly tacking twice in the twenty-four hours somewhere off Buggery Island or the Devil-Tail's Peak."[10]

By their nature men must pursue a goal, Melville holds, but necessary repetition of daily events in the quest disfigures the pursuer and belittles the end. You cannot measure one experience by another because the terms of measurement distort the experience. To measure by external moral standards, as the Christian missionaries did, is fatuous. Then how do you? Or as Montaigne asked, "What do I know?" "Life is so short, and so ridiculous and irrational (from a certain point of view)," Melville wrote his brother-in-law John Hoadley in 1877, "that one knows not what to make of it, unless—well, finish the sentence for yourself."[11] And in the margin of his copy of Matthew Arnold's *Essays in Criticism* he set beside Arnold's quotation from Maurice de Guerin—"The literary career seems to me unreal, both in its essence and in the rewards which one seeks from it, and therefore fatally marred by a secret absurdity"—"This is the finest verbal statement of a truth which every one who thinks in these days must have felt."[12] Deprecating *Redburn* and *White Jacket* in a letter to his father-in-law, he called them jobs done for money. His own "earnest desire" was "to write those sort of books which are said to 'fail.'—Pardon this egotism."[13]

Constant threats of failure and transcendent pride in an enabling vision underpin Dostoevsky's and Melville's courage and self-reliance in extending their literary traditions. Instead of ornamental prose manipulating satiric figures, we find their work to be a new sort of exaggeration—a grotesque account of life, which we are impelled to read by the tension between an apparently objective history of facts and the reality of the protagonist's self-consciousness. The two aspects of perception, akin to an idealist's notions about primary and secondary qualities, are linked not by logic but by compassion, a social metaphorizing in which one man becomes another by taking on his suffering.

The metaphor occurs directly if synesthetically. Valerian Maikov, literary critic and one of Dostoevsky's fellow members in the Petrashevsky Circle, cut through masks and social distortion to say plainly that "the sight of any sore is disgusting, but when you meet it not in the illustrations of a medical article . . . but on the body of a living person in whom you recognize your brother, a second self,—no matter what class he belongs to . . .—love will awaken in you, you will feel that sore on yourself, you will seize your own breast and feel with your own nerves that same pain that brings spasms to your brother's limbs."[14]

It also occurs indirectly. That is, it occurs intellectually, as exemplified by Melville's commenting on the phrase from Emerson's *Essays*, "the good, compared to the evil which he sees, is as his own good to his own evil"—"A Perfectly good being, therefore, would see no evil.—But what did Christ see?—He saw what made him weep.—However, too, the 'Philanthropist' must have been a very bad man—he saw, in jails, so much evil. To annihilate all this nonsense read the Sermon on the Mount, and consider what it implies."[15] If he must choose between truth and Christ, Melville, like Dostoevsky, comes out for Christ. Neither he nor Dostoevsky supposed Christian theology the condition for Christian action.

And the metaphor serves as the ironic basis for a worldview expressed impulsively by Melville in the thought that belief in the existence of a benevolent god makes eternal suffering possible and anxiously by Dostoevsky in the statement that the suffering of one innocent child is unforgivable—that is, inexplicable.

A sharp eye and an honest memory kept bringing Dostoevsky down from utopist, Edenic ideals to the contradictions of everyday life, the literature of which had become popular. For example, by the beginning of Dostoevsky's career in the 1840s, the "poor clerk" theme had become the basis for naturalist writing. Dostoevsky accepted this naturalism as the literary standard, added elements from sentimental and romantic fiction and drama, adapted and twisted it into new forms by idiosyncratic modulation of material and devices from Schiller's plays, Hoffmann's fantastic Berlin tales, Nekrasov's popular *Petersburg Lodgings*, Gogol's demonic, pseudofolkloristic *Evenings on a Farm near Dikanka* and surreal, urban, satiric *Arabesques*. From the beginning, writers and critics regarded him as "the new Gogol." How new they did not know, only sensing that in *Poor People* parody of the rhetorical Gothic novel aligned him with the French *école frénétique* and Jules Janin's *L'âne mort et la femme guillotinée,* a series of stories about a beautiful woman turned into a whore that had appeared in Moscow in 1831, several years before Gogol's "Nevsky Prospect." Natural violence and horrifying plots, as in *The Hunchback of Notre Dame* and works by Balzac, Saintine, and Masson, set the new fiction against the older, idealistic romanticism of Schiller and Schlegel. Reviewing *Dead Souls* in the summer of 1842, Polevoi stood up for the old school: "The waxen description of a rotting corpse, scenes of a drunkard retching and twisting from intoxication—can these really be the subjects of art? . . . Choosing only the dark sides of nature and life, selecting filth, dung, perversity and vice, . . . are you presenting nature and life faithfully?"[16]

By the turn of the century, life and literature were understood differently. In the first quarter of this century, critics began to elaborate the ways in which literary tradition is changed not so much as a reflection of social change as by writers altering literary forms. Tynyanov said, "Any literary succession is, above all, a struggle—the destruction of an old totality and the restructuring of the old elements."[17] He emphasized how Dostoevsky, who adapted many of Gogol's devices, in his early letters played with elements of Gogol's style: "A letter is nonsense; druggists write letters" (1846), or "My letters are a chef-d'oeuvre of *lettristics*" (1844).[18] Respecting letters as literary works, Dostoevsky used them literally in *Poor People* and, throughout his other fiction, as sources for stylistic play in names, actions, plots, and attitude. Beginning with parodic disjunction of comic types, or masks, he, like Melville, proceeded to work up the nuances of dramatic contrast.

It was part of his nature. His whole body dramatized what was in his mind. Tynyanov quotes Strakhov's description of

Dostoevsky's dynamic recitation: "His right hand, convulsively extended downward, was obviously restraining itself from making a suggestive *gesture;* his voice was *raised to a shout.*"[19] In the early fiction, the contrasts were bred by the epistolary and memoir forms. In the later fiction, the contrasts are like shadows heightening the dramatic conflict between plot, on the one hand, and character, on the other. To be said truthfully, a thing must be said obliquely; the figures are seen refracted through the surface of the prose. As Tynyanov put it, "The verbal mask covers a contrasting character,"[20] and cited the parodic opening of *Notes from the Dead House:* "They [the towns] are usually very fully supplied with policemen, superintendents and all the other kinds of minor officials. Generally, serving in Siberia, despite the cold, is exceptionally cushy."[21]

Containing all the elements of Dostoevsky's fiction, the semiautobiographical *Notes from the Dead House* is his first work conceived in fundamental contrasts. Isolated as if in a monastery, the men are cut off from the very pasts for which they are supposedly being punished. Invertedly, the real dramas, like the greatest crimes, occur not in actual life but in their minds.

In Russia, the idea of *type,* now pejoratively an academic cliché, developed from eighteenth-century labeling as a feature of naturalistic writing. A year after *Les Français peints par eux-mêmes* came out in Paris, serving as a kind of manifesto of naturalism, the critic Bulgarin summed up Russian response to the trend: "In Paris it has again become fashionable to make copies from 'originals' . . . but . . . they needed a new word for it, so that instead of the old labels—*morals (moeurs)* and characters (*caractères)*—they took the Greek word *type,* that is, prototype, a first form or *original (original).*"[22] Three years later, after Dostoevsky had translated *Eugénie Grandet*, following Balzac's stay in St. Petersburg, and was at work on his own *Poor People*, the short-story writer Ivan Panayev declared in an essay, "We all use types and regard ourselves as *typical* writers."[23]

In the late 1840s, Dostoevsky was recognized as the leader of "sentimental naturalism," parodist of the type-setters and joke-makers.[24] A decade earlier, Gogol had shown how to write clever, funny stuff in stories like "The Tale of How Ivan Ivanovich Quarreled with Ivan Nikiforovich." So many writers had imitated his style, form, details, devices, and even tone that they had all been dubbed "Gogol's orchestra." In *Poor People*, Dostoevsky adopts but alters Gogol's devices and parodies the "orchestra" in the figure of a writer, Ratazyaev, who announces that he can handle *Italian Passions* and Gothic romance and mimic the descriptive banter of "The Two Ivans."

The comic story had evolved along two lines, as Vinogradov points out. One line was the anecdotal *skaz*, or a series of them, woven into a pattern of grotesqueness emphasizing the discrepancy between a trivial event and its tragic consequences. The other line was portraits, or often caricatures, built by comic typicalization of the attributes of clerks.[25] The long list of those who wrote them includes Dostoevsky's early 1840s, St. Petersburg roommate, Grigorovich, who used slapstick for obvious effect: In his story "The Lottery Ball," clerk Kuvyrkov's pants suddenly fall down.

Very rapidly the rationalizing of comic structure more than modified romantic idealism and naturalistic pathos. As the editorialist of the first issue of *The Fatherland Notes* argued in 1843, by *ideal* the new writers "now understand not an exaggeration, not a lie, not childish fantasy but a real fact as it really is, a fact not copied from real life but conveyed through the poet's imagination, illuminated by the light of general meaning . . . and therefore truer, more faithful to itself than the most slavish copy of real life." Before exile to Siberia and after, Dostoevsky, like Melville in all his work before the Civil War and after, was trying to align the grammar of literature with perceived social change.

Modification meant, first, literary modification—discovery, revision, further experimentation and recombination. Thematically, for example, the insignificant clerk became a man of noble ideals and majestic ambition, as in Yakov Butkov's *Petersburg Heights,* a collection of stories about lodgers in attics and upstairs maids' rooms that preceded *Poor People.* Grigorovich's story "The Theater Carriage" took its structure from Gogol's "The Overcoat," but Grigorovich changed the plot "by making the 'humane' episode the dramatic climax," Vinogradov said, through a comic convention simultaneously achieving emotional coloring and intellectual meaning. Art, or the formal arrangement of experience, is as real as life. It represents facts, and it presents understanding. It concentrates life, draws it into meaning. As Dostoevsky wrote in *The Idiot,* "Writers . . . mostly try to select social types and to present them vividly and artfully—types extremely rarely met as such in real life but nonetheless almost more real than life itself. . . . In real life the typicalness of any figure seems watered down; all the George Dandins and Podkolyosins really do exist, do dream and run around every day before our eyes but as if in somewhat diluted form."

In writing *Poor People,* his first tale of a copy clerk, Dostoevsky discovered in the mid-1840s what Melville discovered in the mid-1850s—how to make an insignificant man importantly human by giving him an idiosyncratic style. Older writers, like Konstantin Aksakov, and critics, like Pavel Annenkov, noted Dostoevsky's conscious artfulness distorted the clerk's "style" and used such a figure as the tailor in "An Honest Thief" as, what Annenkov called, "an instrument for a kind of narrative *tour de force.*"

A new style meant a new set of ideas—in fact, a repatterning of old ideas in such a way that they became new. In his letter of April 12, his third to her, Devushkin asks Varenka not to be hard on him for the way he writes: "I have no style, Varenka, none at all. If only I had some kind of one!" The literature he responds to gradually shapes his style until he becomes a writer himself, his careful penmanship turning into what he calls "the good style of my compositions."

Later in the nineteenth century, in the decadent phase of romanticism, stylishness became a pose, and the process of writing became its own subject, but Dostoevsky and Melville's dramatic romanticism projected style as an aspect of consciousness. The act of writing brings ideas into being, thereby giving reality to the actor and to everyday objects and events. By doing what he imagines, a man enlarges himself. Ultimately, all parts of all worlds are interchangeable through his acts of imagination, that is, through his metaphors, which in one artifice connect spheres of different sizes and of different kinds.

In a letter to Duyckinck shortly before Christmas 1850, Melville turns his Berkshire house into a square-rigger: "I have a sort of sea-feeling here in the country, now that the ground is all covered with snow. I look out of my window in the morning when I rise as I would out of a port-hole of a ship in the Atlantic. My room seems a ship's cabin; & at nights when I wake up & hear the wind shrieking, I almost fancy there is too much sail on the house, & I had better go on the roof & rig in the chimney."[26]

That is the psychology of Dostoevsky's Man in the Cellar, too, but even more of the Siberian population of *Notes from the Dead House,* in which the prison, like the ship, becomes home—not "the bright, free world beyond the gates where ordinary people live" but "a sort of unrealizable fairy tale, very special world like no other, with its own laws, costumes, morals and customs—a house buried alive . . . and the people special." The prisoners self-confidently insist that they are literate and that the past is irrelevant; one does not discuss it. None repents. Most feel they were in the right. Although they have been imprisoned for what they have done, in prison they are what they can become. The metaphoric height is achieved in the theatrical presentation at Christmas, a story within a story creating a tension that binds literary, symbolic significance and philosophic meaning.

The redemptive terms of monastic life derive from its voluntary base—a monk wills himself toward transcendent goodness. In prison, the men are compelled to live and work together. "Monastic life," Sergei Levitsky wrote not long after Dostoevsky's death, "is not an absolute denial of social life; on the contrary, in years of disaster, activists went forth from the monasteries who were really heroes and fighters for the national ideal. The monastery has often thus served the welfare of the people and the state, and Mr. Dostoevsky is certain that a great role lies before it in the life of the people."[27]

Not for the prison. Prison is harmful; at best, pointless. Prisoners' attitudes toward food, flogging, misfortune, or fate in *Notes from the Dead House* are stunningly similar to those of the sailors in *White Jacket.* Like Jack Chase, captain of the foremast, Akim Akimych is a self-taught, self-reliant jack-of-all-trades, a man of ferocious integrity in a world in which "the ability not to be surprised at anything was the supreme virtue." In him style, function, and virility are one. Because of the high purposefulness of his distortion and his concept of justice, he can seem ridiculous—"The prisoners made fun of him"—without losing his dignity. A junior officer, he comes from a higher social standing than most convicts, and he is tall, scrawny, and full of incongruities. Laughter effectively bridges the distance between the excellence beneath his foolish inconsistencies and the other men's ideas of themselves.

Irreconcilable discrepancies underlie *Poor People,* Dostoevsky's 1846 epistolary novel between Varenka Dobrosyolova and Makar Devushkin. Vinogradov's 1924 essay, "The Sentimental Naturalist School," dexterously shows how Dostoevsky's consciousness of style on three levels advanced the literary tradition he had inherited by mimicking, parodying, and reversing its terms. Varenka not only tells her sentimental story of the dishonored country maid in the capital but also accurately reports the defective, colloquial, comical diction of Devushkin and others. Devushkin not only sets himself off from fellow lodgers and clerks but also, friend and admirer of the writer Ratazyaev, compares his own tale "Boots" to Gogol's "The Overcoat," in so doing appropriating for description of himself with socialist commentary the very features he criticizes in Gogol. As Vinogradov wrote, "Makar Devushkin, flaunting his clerical style modeled on Gogol's originals, in the name of all 'titular counselors' and 'poor people' in general, not only sanctioned new trends in the heart of the 'naturalist' school, breaking its obsolescent forms and parodying 'the literary lice,' but also stepped forward as one of the leading, most talented heralds and creators of new artistic forms."[28]

Devushkin's literary quest is a metaphor for Dostoevsky's own, interweaving the two characters' stories by their responses to the seasons' changes and to time past and time future associated with them, Varenka's "golden childhood" and Devushkin's dream of literary fame. Tone and emotional coloring present the figures in contrast to their environment and to each other. The glasslike illusion of happiness with which they begin shatters on the facts of life: At the end, Varenka dwells on her foreboding "that I'll die this Fall," announces her marriage to another, and leaves Devushkin a foresaken, funereal lover. The literary architectonics support the idylls of the imagination.

In *Notes from the Dead House,* the literary framing is simpler. Dostoevsky pretends to offer the notes of Alexander Goryanchikov, imprisoned for ten years for murdering his wife. Because the central idea is stronger and the philanthropic message is ironic and clear, the forms are a freer series of interlocking episodes and character studies. The contrast between *inner* and *outer*, between *here* and *there,* is omnipresent. These metaphysical contraries magnify the verbal tensions of diction and style, as if the least detail expressed ultimate truth. It is a question not of theological argument or of religious symbolism but of projecting spiritual dynamics.

In an essay on Christian themes in American fiction, Denham Sutcliffe pointed out that whores and saints are appealing figures to novelists, that "treatment is everything," that Willa Cather's Catholicism idealized the past without illuminating the struggle for spiritual perfection, and that "no fiction achieves greatness because of its theme."[29] Christ figures are found in modernist Hemingway (*The Old Man and the Sea,* "Today Is Friday") and Faulkner (*The Sound and the Fury, Light in August*) as well as in Bret Harte ("The Luck of Roaring Camp"), Lew Wallace (*Ben-Hur*), and many other sentimental fictionalists. Sutcliffe noted that the fictional world of the most pervasively American writer, Hawthorne, does not include the central Christian idea of redeeming grace. Hawthorne's metaphors are Christian, but his emphasis is psychological in what he called "a world of marble and of mud," a world in which men cannot not sin. "The unforgivable crime is *secret* sin," Sutcliffe commented, "but it is nature—*human* nature—that cries out for confession, not God."[30]

A few years earlier, Evdokimov had come to a similar conclusion about Dostoevsky's work: "Dostoevsky's great master, Saint Isaac the Syrian, insists on the vision of inner Hell: 'He who has seen his sin is greater than he who raises the dead. . . . ' Dostoevsky's synthetic method allows him to combine Job, the Apocalypse, Saint Isaac, a newspaper article, a crime, a street scene in unequalled prose continuity—the mystery novel."[31]

In *Notes from the Dead House* Dostoevsky makes the same psychological argument as Hawthorne but posits a human nature capable of savage insensitivity and comprehensible only in aesthetic terms—for example, the dissipated nobleman who, to inherit a fortune, sliced off his father's head, concealed the body, its head laid on a pillow, denied the deed, and in prison even spoke of his father's "excellent health till the day he died." On the other hand, it is a human nature capable of conscious self-sacrifice or transcendence—for example, the ten-year-old girl who weeps for her dead soldier-father in the ward where Goryanchikov is ill, sees Goryanchikov and, having gotten a quarter-kopek from her mother, gives it to him "in the name of Christ." The past does not matter: The girl does not care why Goryanchikov is there; she cares about his condition. And the prisoners scorn the parricide not because of his crime but because he does not know how to behave.

In the Dead House there are three times: Sentenced and fettered for what they have done, the prisoners psychologically retaliate by escaping from the past into the present, their double nature made plausible by the author's long view from the future. The writer keeps a delicate balance between the psychological reality of what Melville called man's horological time and the ideal chronometry of God.

Joseph Conrad wrote Cunninghame Graham that "crime is a necessary condition of organized life. Society is essentially criminal—or it wouldn't exist."[32] Such disillusioned romanticism, reaching back more than a century to Rousseau, would seem to make Conrad and Dostoevsky both existentialists after all, but by studying criminals Dostoevsky demonstrated that the standard definitions of morality no longer applied. *Crime* and *sin* were not one, and the values according to which social life was organized were not those underlying an adequate definition of human nature. To define *reality* the very concepts of time and space had to be changed.

In Dante's vision, Hell is time past. Present-tense earthly life is but the vestibule to the Heavenly Mansion, the "world of bliss." "Hope is a certain expectation of future glory," the poet says in the *Paradiso* Canto XXV,[33] "the product of divine grace and precedent merit." Illuminated by hope, the blessed transcend themselves, activated by "the love that moves the sun and the other stars."[34] Condemned to hopelessness, the sinners in Hell have become the substance of their sin.

The hell that Dostoevsky describes is an allegorical perversion of society in which we see, as under a magnifying glass, how the least advantage affords gross comfort, how "money is coined freedom." Henry James said that the only reason for the existence of a novel was that it attempted to represent life; the picture here is larger than life. As in *The Inferno*, men condemn themselves by their willed acts, but they do not have to abandon their free will. Although their terms of exile are as fixed as the sailors' terms of shipboard passage, from day to day the end of the term is so remote that it seems a mirage. The men exist in a world that psychologically has neither beginning nor end. Their psychological world has become their real world. As Dostoevsky jotted in his notebook, "In this world, nothing begins and nothing ends."[35]

Chained to each other, compelled to live communally, locked in the present, the convicts, like the *Neversink*'s crew, fear rod and whip, are obsessed with food, and through their language reperceive and redefine themselves. As Goryanchikov says, "They cursed subtly and artfully." To be sure, there are types—the revered, the heroic, the foolish—and there are scapegoats—especially the women who peddle white rolls and their bodies—but most of the men contain inconsistencies that no objective terms adequately embrace. Osip the smuggler is a man "of rare honesty and humility." Frustrating expression of their inconsistencies, repressive prison life distorts their natures. Furthermore, the punishment, a social measure, does not fit the crime, an individual impulse. There is no discernible or believable correlation between cause and effect. To think that there is, is to think conventionally and inadequately. Above all, there is the towering irony that punishment is a crime against human nature. The state is a greater criminal than the prisoners. Imprisonment is unjustifiable. Prison is a place in which the long, dull days pass as monotonously as water drips from eaves after a rain and in which, amid hundreds in a huge anthill, each man lives in terrifying spiritual isolation: "How much youthful energy lay buried pointlessly inside these walls; what great strength here perished for nothing! Because we want to say everything—because these people were extraordinary people. Perhaps the most gifted and the strongest in our whole country. But their great powers perished for nothing, perished abnormally, illegally, irrecoverably. Who's to blame? That's it: Who?"

Social institutions are too cumbersome and too inflexible for one man to change. Those who control them cannot change them, as the sensitive colonel of engineers ("our eagle") who treats the prisoners as human equals can do no more than ease their labor, let them return to barracks early. Those who try to escape the control become more and more immured. As long as the prisoners thought that Kulikov and A-v had escaped, they glorified them; after the two men were captured, the prisoners reviled them: "To the extent that Kulikov and A-v had previously been celebrated, they were now put to shame, put to shame with a vengeance. . . . Success makes all the difference to people."

They also fail who dumbly climb the institutional ladder, like the cruel, overbearing officer who, calling himself "a major by God's grace," perverted divine authority and lost his own when his service record caught up with him. Inside or outside the prison, structure is inhuman. One's real life, like one's worth, is defined by one's moral qualities, which can be abstracted from daily life and seen in artistic representations. Similarly, the prisoners can be ranked not by their crimes but by their virtues, and the meaning of life affirmed by a group of plays at Christmas.

The holiday preparations were special, calling forth prayers and lustrations, geese and suckling pigs, an exceptional spirit of friendliness among the convicts, and bread and foods baked "for the unfortunates" by local merchants' wives. Vodka and singing accompanied the feast. When it was over, "sorrow, sadness and haziness flickered despairingly in the drunken merry-making. . . . Lord, what a heavy and sorrowful day that was for almost everybody. Everybody seemed to be falsely hoping for something."

The first presentation in the prisoners' theater took place on the third day of Christmas. The act of preparing it with the authorities' tolerance kept order in the prison, so that during the holiday season there were no vicious quarrels or thievery. Dostoevsky presents this not as allegory but as fact. Their word of good behavior honored, the convicts who take part in the play become unrealistically optimistic about the extent of their success. Believing wholly in their play making (the first was "Filatka and Miroshka, the Rivals"; the second, "Kedril the Glutton" carried off to Hell by evil spirits; and the third, a musical pantomime), they become childlike and idealistic, exemplifying the most Christian aspects of their natures. Goryanchikov explains at length that the material for the plays and the histrionic attitude supporting them lay deep within the national character or what he calls "the popular theater," meaning amateur groups, former serf theaters, and itinerant players, all of whom handed down oral traditions and unpublished texts.

The staging took place in a barracks fifteen paces long.

Hanging across the middle, separating stage from audience, was an oil-painted curtain stitched from odd pieces of canvas, a miracle of the imagination depicting "trees, gazebos, ponds and stars"—a version of Eden. Goryanchikov, a former officer with some money, sets himself apart and, therefore, functions as a natural observer to whose eyewitness account we readers respond with heightened involvement.

The room is packed. All convicts feel that the theater is theirs. A couple of violins and guitars and three balalaikas make magical music. As the curtain rises, mouths hang open, eyes widen, silence reigns. Perceiving the event's power through its effect, like measuring a horse's strength by the stone weight it can drag, Goryanchikov notes that the theatrical fills the men with "the most naïve, impassioned expectation of miracles and delights." The face of the man beside him shines "with beautiful, childlike joy." The actors do not present clichéd figures. On the contrary, the power of "Filatka and Miroshka" comes from Baklushkin's naturalistic acting, projecting a realistic *muzhik.*

Costumes have been patched together. In this peasant love story as old as Greek romance, men take women's roles ("Sirotkin dressed as a girl was very sweet"). But truth comes alive. As Goryanchikov tells it, the allegorical aspect is dwarfed by descriptions of the men's expressions, their clothing, sounds, and movements and by his own intense psychologizing, establishing a tension between the facts of convict life on the one hand and, on the other, natural goodness and standards of excellence. From behind the clowning, the buffoonery, and the improvisation comes a passionate projection of the spiritual community to which all belong and from which each man draws his strength.

A sort of Don Giovanni and Leporello's last supper, the

second play introduces the sins of gluttony and pride. Devils appear as agents of punishment.

The musical pantomime tells of a miller pursuing his wife's three lovers. It is followed by improvisational scenes, including a resurrection. Revived as he is being buried, a "dead" man gets up and dances. All then join in a ballet.

Like "The Old Wagon Paid Off" acted on board the *Neversink* to celebrate July 4, these theatricals transform actors and audience. The actors come from the audience, but they speak so truthfully that, even when it laughs at them, the audience sees itself in them, which is to say that it sees its best and happiest self. After the plays, as if having reached Heaven, compensated and realized, the men are blissful: "All are unusually pleased, even rather happy, and fall asleep not as they regularly do but with a feeling of peace—and you wonder why. It's not a figment of my imagination. It's real, the real truth. Give these poor men the slightest chance to live as they want, to enjoy themselves as human beings, to spend only an hour in a non-prison way—a man changes morally, even if only for a few minutes."

A man's snoring, another man's rattling his chains remind Goryanchikov that he is not dreaming. This is life. The last thing he hears that night, as he lays his head back on his pillow and thinks of time to come, is an old man on the stove praying, "Jesus Christ, have mercy on us!" Then he, too, completes his role and joins the others in heavenly sleep.

"Even if only for a few minutes," the distorting mirror of make-believe and the clown's masquerade have resolved the contradictions and inconsistencies of an intolerably unjust world.

8

Making, Doing, Thinking

In life everything is counterpoint.
—*Glinka*

BY MODIFYING POPULAR LITERARY FORMS and adapting them to express a comprehensive worldview buttressed by a metaphysic, Dostoevsky and Melville created new realities. In *Illusions perdues,* his portrait of the corrupt Parisian literary world of the late 1830s and early 1840s, Balzac had the hero Lucien de Rubempré observe that "thought arises from the collision of words." In his study of Dostoevsky's Petersburg essays, Komarovich points out how Dostoevsky altered the function and scope of light fiction and social commentary by making the language capable of including previously inaccessible material:

> [In the second feuilleton] the analysis of "filthy poverty" is built entirely on differences in the meaning of the word *filth,* the same device of verbal punning used for personifying Petersburg [in the first feuilleton]. In order to turn Petersburg into a new, separate figure, Dostoevsky used simply the duality of meaning and grammatical signs inherent in the city's name—Petersburg-the-city and Petersburg-the-citizens. With elusively subtle consistency, Dostoevsky creates a third something—his own fantastic iconography.[1]

Melville modified the adventure tale. In a Robinson Crusoe–like way, as *The Spectator* reviewer of 1846 pointed out, Melville manipulated details for comic, dramatic, and symbolic effects, the symbolic being the most important. It showed "the manner in which the isolated individual reacts to a situation of possible permanent isolation," said Faith Pullin, who emphasized Melville's nonrealistic style, the narrative action in *Typee* induced "by the movement of Tommo's mind . . . set in a Douanier-Rousseau type landscape."[2] The mixed method underlines the deceptiveness of appearances and the relativity of cultural values.

In chapter 33 of *The Confidence-Man* Melville asserts that art is high-tension play between what is and what is not:

> It is, indeed, strange . . . that anyone, who, for any cause, finds real life dull, should yet demand of him who is to divert his attention from it, that he should be true to that dullness.
>
> There is another class, and with this class we side. . . . In books of fiction, they look not only for more entertainment, but, at bottom, even for more reality, than real life itself can show. . . . It is with fiction as with religion: it should present another world, and yet one to which we feel the tie.[3]

In *Mardi*, under the influence of books read in Evert Duyckinck's library or borrowed from the New York Society Library, of which he became a member in January 1848, Melville began moving toward creation of his own world of presentation. Documentation of shipboard life establishes the actuality of the microcosm (on the quest for Yillah, each island is an occasion), but the invented, literary characters—King Media the mediator, Babbalanja the philosopher, Mohi the historian, and Yoomy the poet—allow the sailor-author to become Taji the sun god, maker of metaphor, and chronicler of allegory, the one who travels among men to link the islands of the mind while the group travels among Mardi's islands. For all the romance and allegory, the island voyaging is both a chapter-by-chapter tour of the contemporary social world and an improvisation by the author. In *Mardi* and in Poe's "Narrative of A. Gordon Pym," Richard

Brodhead found rejection of ordinary reality, dislocation of self in time and space, violations of taboos, and so forth. In the first half of the first volume, Melville "like Poe . . . is using the form of adventure narrative to conduct an exploration into other modes of reality. . . . The section . . . that follows takes as its model the anatomy form that Melville would have been familiar with in Swift [Book 3 of *Gulliver's Travels*] and Rabelais [Book 4 of *Gargantua and Pantagruel*]."[4] Ultimately, all commentators agree, *Mardi* becomes its own world: The central adventure is the creative process itself. "Taking a book off the brain," Melville later joked in a letter to Duyckinck, "is akin to the ticklish & dangerous business of taking an old painting off a panel."[5]

Taji's monomaniacal quest for Yillah and refusal to accept his guilt when his friends drown involve panels of allegory, discourses on democratic intolerance, even a one-act play, or mock *Symposium,* on literary structure. Social analyses of conditions in the United States, England, and Europe are less important than the attempt to define the principles according to which the book of commentary itself was generated. Even as he leaned backward to imitate eighteenth-century debating rhetoric, Melville focused on his self-consciously literary originality. Brodhead said baldly that Melville was a writer who "compulsively engages in ontological heroics. . . . The true significance of *Mardi* is that it is the first draft of all his subsequent works."[6] To make him a prophet of postmodernism, a writer "obsessed, above all, with 'pure style' and the sheer possibilities of fabulation,"[7] however, is exceptionally to distort his novelistic attitude, according to which he clearly saw evil as the chronic malady of the universe and demanded that his vision of reality be set against God's—that is, against things as they are. "Perhaps, after all, there is *no* secret," he wrote Hawthorne. "But it is this *Being* of the matter; there lies the knot with which we choke ourselves. As soon as you say *Me,* a *God,* a *Nature,* so soon you jump off from your stool and hang from the beam."[8]

Like Jacques Derrida 125 years later, Melville rejected abstract polarities and binary logic, insisting that for language the ironies and paradoxes of discourse contain the only plausible truths. "It is a question posed on the crossing of paths," Derrida wrote, "a question of bifurcation or of bifurcation squared, a question of the crossroads, where each way marked with a stone becomes double, triple, quadruple."[9] The way in is to agree that opposites are unworkable conventions—that *B* supplements *and* replaces A, that there cannot be anything outside a text because a textual structure, like other closed systems, presupposes only itself, and that understanding is reached by disassembling the text.

I think Melville would have thought Derrida's postmodernism rather like taking a huge clock apart to understand the nature of time. I am sure that in *Mardi* his poet Lombardo is autobiographical: " 'Here we are at last, then!' he cried; 'I have created the creative.' "[10] Not only in chapter 180, which discusses Lombardo's "Koztanza," but also throughout *Mardi,* figures are not canceled by being paired off so much as they are projected through their negative. Potential so informs actual, and we readers so perceive absence through presence, that we might well assert that the absence is in the presence. Simply, Melville adapts to the analogical method of metaphoric literature Aristotle's fundamental assumption that a thing is itself by virtue of its not being everything else. Aristotle asserted four classes of subject/predicate meanings expressed as the four kinds of questions we ask, the four kinds of things that we know:

"(1) whether the connexion of an attribute with a thing is a fact; (2) what is the reason of the connexion; (3) whether a thing exists; and (4) what is the nature of the thing."[11] All questions are a search for a "middle," he says; the "middle" is the cause. In syllogistic demonstration, there are attributes that are predicated of a subject essentially or naturally; others, only coincidentally. Saying "That white thing is a man" is not the same mode of predication as saying "The man is white": "The man is white not because he is something else but because he is man, but the white is man because 'being white' coincides with 'humanity' within one substratum."[12] A body can be defined by its whiteness but not whiteness by any body.

By verbal doublings back, by extensive paronomasia, by antiqued diction, fragmentations, and irregular rhythms (such as turning discussion of the "Koztanza" into the quintessential colloquy that a drama is), Melville upset established categories of thinking.

In the chapter "The Whiteness of the Whale" in *Moby-Dick,* Melville assimilates shades of white things beginning with the loveliness of Oriental japonicas and pearls, including figures from Greek, Roman, and Iroquois theology, and culminating in Revelation's white robes of the redeemed, the elders "before the great white throne, and the Holy One that sitteth there white like wool." Associated with "any object terrible in itself," the thought of whiteness heightens "that terror to the furthest bounds." To the Peruvian Indian, the white-capped Andes threaten "inhuman solitudes"; to the sailor, the Antarctic scenery "seems a boundless church-yard grinning upon him with its lean ice monuments and splintered crosses." As a Vermont colt is frightened by the muskiness of a buffalo hide, so Ishmael is appalled by whiteness:

"Though in many of its aspects this visible world seems formed in love, the invisible spheres were formed in fright." To behold the Milky Way is to be stabbed "with the thought of annihilation."[13]

Insofar as Locke and the empiricists correctly assigned secondary qualities to the mind, then all nature—all that *is*—is a deceitful covering, a refraction of white light that is really no color itself but without which the world would be colorless—that is, formless. Like a paradox, whiteness embodies absence in presence. As Melville asked in that same chapter, "Is it, that as in essence whiteness is not so much a color as the visible absence of color, and at the same time the concrete of all colors; is it for these reasons that there is such a dumb blankness, full of meaning, in a wide landscape of snows—a colorless, all-color of atheism from which we shrink?"

In *White Jacket,* the whiteness is called "a universal absorber." Through its functions in the narrative, the jacket becomes a multivalent symbol. It is an end in itself, but also it is used to find something else, preparing for the quest for whiteness that establishes the textual tension in *Moby-Dick,* a book whose power derives from the fact that the object of Ahab's desire is undiminishedly the author's generative obsession. The whale and the ship, like the paradox and its author, circle each other perfectly. Neither exists without the other; indeed, each exists through the other.

This is crudely adumbrated in the penultimate playlet in *Mardi*; social commentary and anagogical truthfulness, however, are separate. Babbalanja expatiates, "There are things infinite in the finite, and dualities in unities. Our eyes are pleased with the redness of the rose, but another sense lives upon its fragrance. . . . So with Koztanza. Its mere beauty is restricted to its form: its expanding soul past Mardi does embalm. Modak is Modako; but fogle-foggle is not fugle-fi."[14] Although the two kings hang their crowns up like hats and honesty among intelligent men brings forth bright conversation, the luxury of idleness does not guarantee either intimacy or understanding. Lombardo the author has been tormented by self-doubt—had he the talent to match his ambition: "Ah, Oro! How may we know or not, we are what we would be?"[15] As it breaks up, the group splinters in response: The historian admits having ignored the poem; the poet is pleased to have discussed it; one king never read it, and the other read it nine times; the philosopher, who led the talk, ignores its content and praises Lombardo's intent. "Evil is the chronic malady of the universe,"[16] the Vivenza scroll read, and Babbalanja has previously expressed the paradoxical terms of truthfulness: "There is no place but the universe, no limit but the limitless, no bottom but the bottomless."[17]

In *Moby-Dick* Melville guides a reader into that world through the "Etymology" and the "Extracts"; in *White Jacket* his opening sentences bring a reader literally to the jacket, which Melville then complicates as a symbol by a physical transformation analogous to, or imitative of, a literary: "It was nothing more than a white duck frock, or rather shirt; which, laying on deck, I folded double at the bosom, and by then making a continuation of the slit there, opened it lengthwise—much as you would cut a leaf in the last new novel. The gash being made, a metamorphosis took place, transcending any related by Ovid. For, presto! the shirt was a coat!"[18]

The imaginative act making something more out of something else gives us a jacket "white enough," "strange-looking," "white as a shroud," "a burden," "a universal absorber," "an albatross," "an old castle," the keeper of "foul weather" that symbolizes Melville's narrative of a young man's three-stage romance with the world: His initiation into evil; his reflections on it and revulsion from it; his baptism in it. The jacket is the man, and the man is the ship, giving it life by his functioning. The *Neversink* is homeward bound to the Edenic "green old clime; the old arching elms." But such is the irony of evil that the one honest man on board, who cannot get paint to waterproof his jacket, appears as the nemesis: Loosing the main-royal as the ship gets under way, Whitejacket "was taken for an albatross himself."[19]

Later in the tale, Melville declares that "a ship is a bit of terra firma cut off from the main; it is a state in itself; and the captain is its king."[20] The men are the people in a special utopia without private property or personal privacy, a world in which the "Declaration of Independence is a lie." Isolated in their floating world, they are set apart from other time exactly as if they were in Siberia. *No Sundays off soundings,* as the seaman's maxim says. We sailors "expatriate ourselves to nationalise with the universe." Almost all their efforts on board are for working the ship, struggling with nature. The act of will and the reason behind it that made each man sign on are as irrelevant to shipboard life as crime is to punishment: "The Navy is the asylum for the perverse, the home of the unfortunate. Here the sons of adversity meet the children of calamity, and here the children of calamity meet the offspring of sin."[21]

The ship is "a city afloat," a lofty walled town, a Paris lodging-house, a "three-storey house in a suspicious part of the town," indeed even a church with three spires, three steeples, a bell, and a belfry. It imitates or embodies all social institutions, sometimes inverting, sometimes telescoping the top and the bottom. When there is no work to do, when the men are "killing time in harbour," the author feels most imprisoned and discovers a goodness, common to the crew "all under lock and key; all hopeless prisoners like myself; all under martial law; all dieting on salt beef and biscuit; all in one uniform; all yawning, gaping, and stretching in concert, it was then that I used to feel a certain love and affection for them, grounded, doubtless, on a fellow-feeling."[22]

From this lyrical immurement he shifts to Shakings's story, the ex-Sing-Sing convict and fore-holder who liked reminiscing with ex-inmates and who in difficult moments wished himself not forward ashore to things worth living for beyond the man-of-war world but back into his snug, safe, guarded cell "where he was relieved from all anxieties about what he should eat and drink, and was supported, like the President of the United States and Prince Albert, at the public charge."[23] Shakings "scandalously" asserts the man-of-war "to be a sort of state prison afloat." Melville takes the thinking to an ultimate end, asserting that the earth itself is just such a vessel. It may well be, he says, that some disposition to fraternize and be sociable such as moved the ex-convicts "shall hereafter fraternally reunite all us mortals, when we shall have exchanged this state's prison man-of-war world of ours for another and a better."[24]

Psychologically, man swings between submission and control. The sea uses him harshly; men use each other worse. But "man can become used even to the hardest voyage," says Melville the narrator, as Dostoevsky has Raskolnikov in *Crime and Punishment* say, "Man's a scoundrel gets used to anything!" then reflect a moment and burst out wondering, "What if man is not actually a *scoundrel*? I mean, if the human species isn't, why then everything's just prejudices, nothing but exaggerated fears, and there are no limits, and that's how it's meant to be!"[25]

For Melville's narrator, the wondrous obverse is the "influence of habitual sights and sounds upon the human temper," the ways in which man can bring himself into harmony with his world. Melville is under no illusion that man often does so or that all men can. The standard is set by the hero, Jack Chase the "saving genius" of the ship rounding Cape Horn, the star of the shipboard play, the man of the people. Lemsford's integrity as a poet is measured not by his shore-published chapbook but by calling Jack a man of the people in response to Jack's enthusiastic irony after Lemsford's manuscript "Songs of the Sirens" has been shot out of its hiding place in cannon No. 20. "The public is one thing, Jack," says Lemsford, "and the people, another."[26] The people necessarily draw together in their suffering, even through the suffering that glorifies the commodore. The novelist's task is to offer a view of man and a vision of justice compatible with possibility. To do that he must reuse words to create an inverted hierarchy, much as the sailors, playing with checkers, imitate and escape from the ways the officers repress them.

Melville's favored device is some form of paronomasia, usually punning, a self-regulating process in which syntactical arrangement binds the shifts of meaning. Mistaken aloft for the cooper's ghost and nearly tumbled from the rigging, Whitejacket hurls his jacket on deck and addresses it in eighteenth-century style as if it were his double: " 'Jacket,' cried I, 'you must change your complexion! you must hie to the dyer's and be dyed, that I may live. . . . I cannot consent to die for *you,* but be dyed you must for me. You can dye many times without injury; but I cannot die without irreparable loss.'"[27] The old-fashioned punning breaks through conventional thinking, liberates the mind from unnecessary quilting.

At the end of the narrative, Whitejacket falls from the yardarm, saves his life by separating himself from his double: "I whipped out my knife . . . and ripped my jacket straight up and down, as if I were ripping open myself. With a violent struggle I then burst out of it, and was free." The sailors who earlier thought the jacket a ghost now think it a white shark and harpoon it to the bottom. Thus are practical men ever shortsighted, required to act whether defensively or generously on information no amount of experience can show them is inadequate.

The world of the ship, like the white jacket and the sea into which it falls, is not more physical than emblematic of consciousness. Rhetorically, Melville makes point after point (a reason that his ideas, like Dostoevsky's, are readily debated), but the authenticity of perceived detail makes the structure credible. Leon Howard has documented that the comic episodes—the theatricals, the fall overboard, the beard-trimming, and so on—all were taken from James Mercier's *Life in a Man-of-War, or Scenes in Old Ironsides,*[28] showing once again that Melville often drew his material from other men's experiences. In *White Jacket,* however, he imagines himself into those experiences in broad perspective with firsthand intimacy. For example, he digresses from Whitejacket's fall—a matter of seconds—to give us half a dozen paragraphs on perceptions connected with falling; so, when the jacket goes into the water, we go, too. That is the "real" fall, no matter what arc of relativity Whitejacket described from the foretop yard to the sea abeam the mizzenmast. The conclusions drawn from the fall show how much better a representation of the world the ship is than the islands of Mardi.

Dostoevsky acknowledges the Euclidean space of usual urban perspective, but he shapes non-Euclidean space in his actors' consciousnesses, where events presentiently occur. So does Melville: Whitejacket's past goes down with his jacket, as Ahab, going down with the whale, has become his idea of Moby-Dick.

One may then judge these acts morally. Melville's vision requires turning what might have been a moral tract like those popular in midcentury into a philosophic dialogue vibrant with ambiguity and as chaotic as life. Moby-Dick was a "real" whale, untamable, not like those that P. T. Barnum put in his American Museum and made posters of. Sometimes I think that Melville invented a sort of demonic free will for Moby-Dick, the right ultimately to destroy himself and whatever humans and human things he could. As Melville noted in the margin of his *King Lear,* "The infernal nature has a valor often denied to innocence."[29]

In existential terms, exercising free will means acting from desire, not under constraint. So complex is the web of desires that, even if you assume naturalistic determinism, you cannot define a neural or a social cause-and-effect chain. Whatever your assumptions about the nature of free will, an originating impulse lies inscrutably remote in the psychic dark. Events for which there seems to be no adequate causal explanation—what we dismissively call "coincidence"—must, after the fact, appear inevitable, as if fated or preordained. Although we ordinarily attach no importance to them, they are the threads with which we weave the fabric of our lives.

We may learn this from experience; we certainly learn it from Dostoevsky's manipulation of chance to reveal literary motive. There is no *reason* for Raskolnikov to have met the young police clerk Zamyotov in the Crystal Palace restaurant soon after the murders or, indeed, for Raskolnikov to have killed the old pawnbroker's sister. Moving along the orbits of their lives, these people unexpectedly came together in space-time. What matters is what Dostoevsky then makes of the encounters and has the people make of themselves.

To try to preserve both the facts of experience and the conventions of old-fashioned belief, you can declare that such patterns assume and express an irrefutable identity—that every measurable fact asserts an unquestionable origin. Harvard's popular zoologist Louis Agassiz did this. He came from Neuchâtel to Cambridge in 1848, the same year he and Augustus Gould published their *Principles of Zoology,* the first and most widely read text in the field. An anti-Darwinian all his life, Agassiz assumed that the formal cause for everything past, present, and future had long ago been cast:

> In the beginning [God's] plan was formed, and from it He has never swerved in any particular. The same Being who, in view of man's moral wants, provided and declared, thousands of years in advance, that "the seeds of woman shall bruise the serpent's head," laid up also for him in the bowels of the earth those vast stores of granite, marble, coal, salt, and the various metals, the products of its several revolutions; and thus was an inexhaustible provision made for his necessities, and for the development of his genius, ages in anticipation of his appearance. To study, in this view, the succession of animals in time, and their distribution in space, is therefore to become acquainted with the ideas of God Himself.[30]

Like Agassiz, Melville expected mechanical classification to express a spiritual principle. He, too, believed that the source of natural history was supernatural. He wondered at divine power, and he generalized from observation to meaning. But, said Joseph Flibbert, "the conclusions Melville drew . . . contend with those of Agassiz and, accordingly, with those of his age."[31]

In connection with *Moby-Dick,* many commentators have pointed out Melville's literary debts ranging from the Bible and Shakespeare to *Sartor Resartus* and *Mosses from an Old Manse,* and stressed his revisionary skill in moralizing his drama, striking through his own mask and catching his whale. Yet Melville, sensing his ineptness, almost always felt responsible for being out of tune. As he wrote Hawthorne, "What I feel most moved to write, that is banned—it will not pay. Yet, altogether, write the *other* way I cannot. So the product is a final hash, and all my books are botches."[32] His mind stood against Emerson's patrimony, Carlyle's passion, and Goethe's noble purpose—against the greatest literary minds of his day. Like Dostoevsky, he had come full face to the struggle between existential disbelief in man's goodness and religious conviction of man's inherent nobility. Truth, he believed, lies not in knowledge itself but in what we do with our knowledge. In *Moby-Dick* he challenged prevailing assumptions about its value and usefulness. "Physiognomy," the latest semiscience of the 1840s, "like every other human science," he wrote, "is but a passing fable." In a world without limits, only inherited tradition contains the tools for change.

The critic and biographer Raymond Weaver thought Melville an undisciplined writer most interesting "as a tortured and cryptic personality" who "threw himself unreservedly into his creations" and whose "imagination was exclusively a vent for his personal preoccupations."[33] Admiring Melville's aesthetic standard of "sincerity," a standard later taken up by Yeats, Weaver might better have taken Melville straight, who called the Dean Dickson affair in Groton "half melancholy, half farcical—like all the rest of the world."[34]

As Melville saw it, the constant, uneven conflict between these two masks or principles expressed vigor and impermanence in life. Any coordinated set of principles had incomplete relevance. Furthermore, with the passing of time the terms must change, and either a science would prove to be inadequate to the facts or the scientist would have to change his assumptions. Function was everything—form expressed function, like the parts of the great whale and of the ship itself. Horatio Greenough had understood this as early as the 1830s: "Variation is a characteristic of organic rhythm. . . . Visual qualities [comprise] a language . . . whose . . . elements have force from their relation, and not from positive existence."[35]

Melville went farther: All relations being reciprocal, what works one way must also work the other. Immanent in every thing is its opposite. Ahab pursues what he would apotheosize; the whale in him destroys him; and so forth. Farcically speaking, even the "paradise" for which a man longs and in which he has his proper function is an escape from exigency: "With a philosophical flourish, Cato throws himself upon his sword. I quickly take to the ship. This is my substitute for pistol and ball."[36]

Both *Journal up the Straits* and the earlier *Journal of a Visit to London and the Continent* make clear that Melville was an agile sailor, confident, modest, cool, skilled, at home on the sea, a man who "owned" it insofar as use begets proprietorship; but more important is Melville's indirect argument that, since any structure contains its contrary, no structure is absolute. There is no universal yardstick. In Liverpool, he visited Hawthorne, who subsequently jotted down a description of this characteristic: "Melville, as he always does, began to reason of Providence and futurity, and of everything that lies beyond human ken, and informed me that he had 'pretty much made up his mind to be annihilated'; but . . . I think he will never rest until he gets hold of a definite belief. . . . He can neither believe, nor be comfortable in his unbelief; and he is too honest and courageous not to try to do one or the other."[37] Hawthorne's notebook entry echoes the end of "The Fountain" in *Moby-Dick* in which Ishmael speaks about himself: "Doubts of all things earthly, and intuitions of some things heavenly; this combination makes neither believer nor infidel, but makes a man who regards them both with equal eye."

The series of *Pequod*'s gams, like Melville's importunate philosophizing, has tempted commentators to define his work and the ideas in it statically, but I think that Hawthorne's sense of Melville's personal dynamism is closer to our sense of the principle of uncertainty running through *Moby-Dick.* In "The Try-Works," for example, references to Cowper, Young, Pascal, Rousseau, Rabelais, Isaiah, Proverbs, and Ecclesiastes buttress and extend the dramatic fix Ishmael got into when, at the helm, mesmerized by the fire, he turned sternward and nearly lost control of the ship, but the sum of the references is less than the drama. The allegory of human artifice versus natural light, of Satan versus God, seems clear enough (for my taste, too clear), but the book's power, like the references used as divining rods, lies in Melville's continual effort to show the presence of truth without limiting it by locating it: "There is a wisdom that is woe; but there is a woe that is madness."

To be mad is to act outside the limits of manner and meaning, to "wander out of the way of understanding," and to be spiritually dead. Even Solomon's wisdom—"All is vanity"—does not define *the* truth, for there is no way to set a line between "matter and impertinency" when a man and his mind move from divine control to demonic liberty. The perception of changeover will come after the fact and, like Edgar's of Lear, assert irresoluble contraries simultaneously:

> O, matter and impertinency mix'd!
> Reason in madness!

I think Melville's artistic ideal was to express Greenough's organic rhythm as a force celebrating the indefinable.

The parable of brotherhood in squeezing the coagulated spermaceti back into liquid is based on pure sensuality—"I lived as in a musky meadow; . . . in the inexpressible sperm, I washed my hands and my heart of [our horrible oath]"—and on pure Eros—"Let us all squeeze ourselves into each other; let us squeeze ourselves universally into the very milk and sperm of kindness." It is the exaggerated vision toward which the self longs in preservation, directly contradicted by the whale's inscrutable face: "Thou shalt see my back parts, my tail, he seems to say, but my face shall not be seen," an echo of Jeremiah's declaration—

> In the hour of their downfall
> I will turn my back towards them and not my face.[38]

For his part, Melville says that what cannot be seen in words does not exist: "Hint what he will about his face, I say again he has no face."

Between the extremes of self-fulfillment and nonexistence the circle of questing and questioning traces a cycloid, as the soapstone circles the try-pot. *There she blows!* sets the cycle in motion:

> This is man-killing! Yet this is life. For hardly have we mortals by long toilings extracted from this world's vast bulk its small but valuable sperm; and then, with weary patience, cleansed ourselves from its defilements, and learned to live here in clean tabernacles of the soul; hardly is this done when—*There she blows!*—the ghost is spouted up, and away we sail to fight some other world, and go through young life's old routine again.
>
> Oh! the metempsychosis! Oh! Pythagoras, that in bright Greece, two thousand years ago, did die, so good, so wise, so mild; I sailed with thee along the Peruvian coast last voyage—and, foolish as I am, taught thee, a green simple boy, how to splice a rope![39]

To assert immortality or to propose a gigantic metaphor, like Plato's Myth of Er depicting equilibrium between body and soul, requires a belief not credible in the nineteenth century. In the context of a literary structure, however, transmigration becomes possible and plausible. Removed from the limits of the physical world, coincidence becomes fate, motive becomes necessary and sufficient cause. Ordinary-life events sometimes seem to have been previously experienced in dream. Sometimes, from precognition we respond to what has not yet happened.

Either way, we see that an aesthetic structure houses more realities than we experience, and that the "realness" comes from the housing, from the pattern. A home within a house, Melville's ship is an imitation of society set on a literary ocean. He can sail it anywhere words go.

9
Visions and Epiphanies

In Molly all flowers are united.
—*Tindall*

CAST OF MIND SEEMS TO COME FIRST. LITERary talent is fed by a moral typology copied from social institutions. Dostoevsky's creakily plotted *Netochka Nezvanova,* the novel he was working on when arrested in 1849, exposes the difficulty of bringing literary pattern and moral idealism into harmony. After "The Double," he planned the big four-part novel, which he subtitled "The History of a Woman." Scarcely half-done at the time of his arrest, it remained unfinished, though in a revised version included in his collected works.

Autobiographical material is thinly disguised in the opening theme of a musician who, through will-lessness, squanders a great, natural talent and drinks his life away; and in the second theme, that of his stepdaughter Netochka's slavish, sexually sublimated attachment. Netochka narrates her own story. She makes plausible both her stepfather's history and the dumb poverty the family of three stumble through. With acumen and integrity she reports the shifts in the hidden war of love and hate among them, culminating in her agreeing to steal money from her mother for her stepfather to buy a ticket to his erstwhile rival's concert, a theft ironically obviated by the arrival of the prince's man with a free ticket. Initially furious at the theft, the mother suddenly changes her mind and fills with pride that her husband was invited—showing how Dostoevsky steamed the characters together in the pot of poverty, the oppressiveness of their condition driving them to psychological extremes and reversals that simultaneously construct secure aesthetic proportions.

Netochka and her stepfather are bound together not by incestuous feelings but by the rhythm of intimate reciprocity marking their natural antagonism, much as the stepfather turns his fellow opera musicians against him by mocking their taste until they drive him out of the orchestra. Poverty, like a prison, tightly binds the three characters and excludes all others. Within that circle, Netochka's intelligence pierces the placebos of standard morality:

> He couldn't sit still a second and didn't touch a bite, kept getting up every minute and then sitting down again, as if changing his mind, first grabbing his hat as if about to go somewhere, then behaving absentmindedly, muttering to himself, then suddenly staring at me, winking at me, making signs, as if impatient to get the money right away and angry that I hadn't yet taken it from Mother. Even Mother noticed his strangeness and looked at him in surprise. I felt sentenced to death. Dinner came to an end; I hid in my corner and, trembling as if feverish, counted each minute until Mother, as usual, would send me out to do the shopping. . . . I felt I was doing something bad: He himself had helped my good instincts when, like a coward, he had driven me to wickedness the first time and, frightened by it, had explained that I had behaved very badly. Couldn't he see how hard it was to deceive a nature eager to be aware of everything, one that had already experienced and come to understand a lot about good and evil? After all, I knew that it was clearly a terrible extreme which made him dare a second time to drive me to vice and thereby to sacrifice my poor, defenseless childhood innocence, once again dangerously to shake my wobbling conscience. Cringing in my corner, I kept wondering to myself: Why did he promise a reward for what I had decided to do of my own free will?[1]

Broken by life, the mother dies in her bed. The stepfather

grabs Netochka and flees through the streets; a couple of days later, he dies in a frenzy.

After his death, Netochka's attachment is transferred to the little girl in the aristocratic family who bring her up and leads into the novel's third theme—suspected adultery by the woman who has taken over as mother. These three female figures then shift around each other in a mechanical plot. An orphan boy's story, introduced in the version serialized in *The Fatherland Notes* but later deleted, merely parallels Netochka's without extending it. No wonder Dostoevsky cut it, but no cuts could insert into the flat prosperity of the prince's haven the tormented exaggeration that gave roundness and fullness to the world of the poor.

Early in his career, Dostoevsky found narrative voice a means for narrative distortion, a kind of regulator to make apparently inconsequential events vibrate with dramatic power. In the nearly plotless idyll of 1849, "A Little Hero," written in the Peter-and-Paul Fortress, memory houses the struggle between the narrator's compassion and his vision, by its distance imposing on youthful idealism both artistic form and moral pleasure. The climax of the unequal love affair between a young boy and Madame M is a series of reciprocating gestures—a bouquet, a letter, a kiss, a kerchief—delayed by a bee and interrupted by her friends. How the narrator sets himself apart from his past, framing the affair with its own impossibility, supplies the dramatic tension. The longed-for apotheosis, following the ecstatic moment of Madame M's kiss on the lips and the dropped kerchief, is an Edenic vision:

> I tore her kerchief off [my face] and kissed it, beside myself in ecstasy; for a few minutes I was out of my mind! Scarcely catching my breath, leaning on my elbow in the grass, I stared unconsciously and motionlessly ahead at the surrounding hills bright with plowed fields, at the stream meander-

ing among them and, far away, as far as the eye could see, winding in between other hills and villages shimmering like dots in the light-flooded distance, at the dark blue woods seeming to rise in a smoky haze on the edge of the redhot sky, and a sweet peacefulness cast by the triumphant quiet of the scene little by little calmed my excited heart.[2]

In this miniature circling, the self is distinguished by its awareness, and its ideas are bodied forth in things and acts confronting each other, coming to closure without conclusion. The boy asserts himself because he wants her to love him (self-assertion comes from wanting to achieve something; rebellion is an attempt to establish identity), but her attention—the kiss, the kerchief—sufficiently expresses her acceptance on his level of need, and he, in response, accepts the whole world.

A usual interpretation of Dostoevsky's religious ideas, such as Lossky's *Dostoevsky and His Christian World-view,* characterizes Roman Catholicism as unity without freedom, Protestantism as freedom without unity, and Eastern Orthodoxy as freedom in unity/unity in freedom, opposing to the idea of the legal state and its laws as obstacles to freedom the idea of spiritual catholicity. This romantic interpretation, emphasizing the individual's transcendent centrality, links Vasily Rozanov's quasi-mystical *F. M. Dostoevsky's Legend of the Grand Inquisitor* to the secular but no less introverted "God is dead" postmodernists of the 1960s. Critic Michael Holquist considers Dostoevsky's writings apt expression of the mid-nineteenth-century Russian national search for identity. For him, Dostoevsky is a modernist not because of themes of alienation, the death of God, or the transvaluation of values, but because there is "in his work an obsessive meditation on the opposition that generates *all* such preoccupations—the structure—and its transformations—that underlies all 'modern' themes: the conflict between moment and sequence, between modern and historical."[3] Holquist says that Dostoevsky undermined the illusion of individuality by the same sort of questioning that undermined the illusion of man's divinity.

To stay with "structure" and to abandon "themes" leads to a more nearly adequate understanding. "Individuality," "divinity," and similar concepts are not ideas in themselves but confluences of responses within a value system. If we reduce Dostoevsky's writings to his "ideas," we trivialize them. The imagination wants a system made by words, colors, sounds, or mathematical symbols within which to confront the alternatives behind experience. I do not think that any structure independently underlies the conflict between moment and sequence, a conflict that cannot be conceived outside of structural assumptions. I think that the structure itself (for Dostoevsky, the aesthetic and moral use of language) presents to the mind the simultaneous contradictions that cannot otherwise exist.

Dostoevsky is interested not in *now* and *then* but in *now* and *now*. By returning his ticket, Ivan Karamazov stops confronting the intolerable simultaneity that this world is both God's creation and the expression of God's love.[4] Such concepts are inadequate for understanding innocent suffering. As Stewart Sutherland paraphrases the argument of chapter 4, Book 5 of *The Karamazov Brothers*, "If this world is the expression of the love of God for man, what hopes can one hold out for the love of man for man?"[5]

Many readers have been drawn to Ivan's poem by precisely this idea: Given freedom by Christ, man acts independently of God's grace; therefore, the Grand Inquisitor's corruption of the gift is irreproachable. Simply, human suffering comes not *despite* Christ's gift of freedom but *because* of it. Sutherland points out that Dostoevsky's reactionary views in *A Writer's Diary* celebrating human freedom and benevolent autocracy are different from the questions raised and the values asserted in his fiction. Ivan's poem is not an essay about doing good or evil but a dramatization of the terms by which we measure the virtue of "good" and the wickedness of "evil." The Grand Inquisitor's power would justify cynical realism, but as Sutherland says, Dostoevsky himself does not ask the Inquisitor's question, "Was Christ's gift a gift of love?" Looking at the world as it is, Dostoevsky asks, "What difference has it made?" Because the romantic idea of freedom has become obsolete, the important question for him—the one he raises in almost all his fiction and poses through the persona of Ivan—is, "What is the nature of love?"

Ivan's poem is Dostoevsky's most artistically complex and philosophical development of narrative distortion induced by narrative voice. It is a digression from the plot. It is a parable, the import of which is completed by Alyosha's mimetic gesture. It is an anachronistic fantasy. It is a passionate lyric. Above all, it is a histrionic self-confrontation, a confession in which Ivan stages the two sides of himself, or two contradictory assumptions, in one space-time.

In *Netochka Nezvanova* the aesthetic purity of confessional narrative is judged by ideal artistic achievement—the violinist who succeeds *versus* the violinist who fails. Indeed, most of Dostoevsky's stories and novels are first-person narratives either by a participant (the confession) or by an observer (the diary). The narrator begins by alluding to a crucial dilemma that must be solved immediately to avoid terrible consequences, but usually the fiction ends without a final solution. Usually the narrator is the central actor and presents his material as a secret document ("White Nights," *The Adolescent*) or as revealed correspondence (*Poor People*). Always contrasted to what happened is what the narrator dreams—as Varvara in *Poor People* sentimentally contrasts her pathetic humiliation to her happy childhood.

Mikhail Bakhtin has pointed out that the polyphonic structure of Dostoevsky's fiction is based on the author's dialogue with his characters, with whom he does not "identify" but to whom he relates as "the true artist."[6] Usually they are split, often in two as in "The Double," extending the device Poe first used in "William Wilson." In "The Legend of the Grand Inquisitor," Ivan is Dostoevsky's own double, a linguistic blacksmith creating himself and his "reality" through the twinned dialogue expressing consciousness. "If we wanted a picture of reality the sentence itself *is* such a picture," Wittgenstein said, who much admired *The Karamazov Brothers.* "Understanding a sentence means understanding a language"; "understanding a sentence . . . points to a reality outside the sentence."[7]

Dostoevsky's letters to Lyubimov, assistant editor of *The Russian Messenger* in which the Karamazovs' story was appearing serially in 1879, reduce the novel's irresoluble tensions to a moralistic problem. For example, Dostoevsky explained that Ivan's "convictions are precisely what I call the *Synthesis* of contemporary Russian anarchism. The denial not of God but of the significance of what He has created. All socialism has come out of and proceeded from the denial of the significance of historical reality and evolved into a program of destruction and anarchism."[8]

From a writer who kept begging his editor for advances, even that letter introduced the iconoclastic and imaginative independence with which Dostoevsky projected the integrity of unorthodox people: "The principal anarchists were, in many instances, people with sincere convictions. My hero presents a theme *I think* irrefutable: the pointlessness of children's suffering, and from it demonstrates the absurdity of our entire historical reality. I don't know if I've done it well, but I know that the character of my hero is to the highest degree true-to-life."[9] Ten days later in a letter to Pobedonostsev, Dostoevsky said that "madmen have their own logic, their own learning, their own laws, even their own god and are as settled into it as settled can be."[10] Ivan's going mad takes him into that inaccessibility.

In *Notes from the Cellar,* Dostoevsky says that man's soul is not subject to the processes of historical actuality. Good and evil are nonrational. Evil putrefies the spirit, as if turning it into stinking flesh like saintly Zosima's body, but good purifies it. By nature man is good. If his rebellion against the ignorant world's falseness and hypocrisy traps him in corrupting passions, his soul pains him. He suffers remorse. To deny this goodness in himself—to defy God's creation and to assert himself above everything—leads to self-annihilation, the shattering of personality that is madness. A criminal is one who has failed in his quest for self-affirmation and freedom. Because the body is subject to necessity and causality, but the soul can contain contraries and aspire to freedom, in any man's consciousness moral standards must appear relative to his point of view.

Dostoevsky's technique is to isolate each major character in its own single-mindedness and then, in his supreme single-mindedness, by a series of coincidences, analogies, and metaphors to weave an aesthetic pattern. The struggle for freedom is a dialectic, at every stage resolving itself into a further refinement of the dilemma between excellences and vulgarities, but the beautiful is accessible only to excellence—including the excellence of parody, the self-mockery of the grotesque, and the perverseness of the absurd. For example, driven to delirium by his crime, Raskolnikov fears that to Napoleon it would have seemed ridiculous and judges it not a moral but an aesthetic failure. Such faith in the self-sufficiency of a single consciousness, Bakhtin noted, "is a structural characteristic of the ideological creativity of modern times, the determinant of its own inner and outer form."[11] The irony with which "inner" and "outer" play against each other makes Dostoevsky seem even more our contemporary than he was.

A number of his stories deal with children at the voluptuous age when temptation is real: They are aware equally of good and evil and, like Netochka or like the girl Stavrogin violated, are committed to neither. They are innocent, watching the world from a personal, passive point of view. Liza Khokhlakova in *The Karamazov Brothers* is such a teenager, who dreams of devils and has a vision of herself watching a Jewish father chop off his small son's fingers and then crucify him while she eats pineapple compote.

The beginning of self-assertion marks the loss of innocence and is often expressed as adult self-mockery. In *Crime and Punishment,* Marmeladov courts martyrdom and mimics Christ's crucifixion by applying Pilate's "Behold the man!" to himself and by then asking Rasolnikov if he will dare state positively that he, Marmeladov, is not a pig. In the Gospel According to John, the priests cry out for crucifixion; in *Crime and Punishment,* Raskolnikov says nothing, leaving Marmeladov in the disfiguring pathos of his self-awareness and to death by accident. In the same novel, Svidrigailov is the embodiment of the power of contamination—the almost irresistible, mysterious devil of temptation that inhabits every man's subterranean self. Expressed, it seems as grotesque as a gargoyle, but its distortions are self-induced, as Svidrigailov hints by quoting in translation part of the line "I am a man, and nothing human is alien to me" from Terence's play *The Self-Torturer,* the line that in *The Karamazov Brothers* Ivan's gentleman-devil turns into "I am Satan, and nothing human is alien to me." Evil's source lies not in some part of creation untouched by God but in man's very center. For Svidrigailov, as for Kirillov in*The Demons,* the ultimate self-torment or self-temptation is suicide.

Visions, dreams, and sometimes images string together and compound the moral problems. To an intensity unequaled by any nineteenth-century novelist except Melville, Dostoevsky contrasted the holistic artifice of aesthetic construction to the psychological partiality of character. His actors *mean* more than they *do.* No character correctly understands another because no two characters share identical terms or viewpoints. And no one character dominates the action or the presentation of the action. Even in ridiculous stories like "Bobok" or "The Crocodile," Dostoevsky turns material of credible comic conventionality—for example, that the dead in their cemetery coffins converse among themselves, or that a crocodile's belly is a huge galosh—into incredible material revealing the significance of what ordinary men live by.

Set phrases, like running gags, form linguistic actualities. Images turn into patterns. Things reverse. Matters of life and death are treated as games. Make-believe becomes real. Unfinished sentences, hints, looks, and glances create an air of mystery. The shifting point of view, sliding from one character to another, to the reader, to the author, heightens suspense, multiplies interpretations, and establishes parallel levels of narrative. Raskolnikov's story and the Man in the Cellar's, to take two examples, happen equally inside and outside their minds, which are affected by what Ivan Petrovich, the novelist-narrator of *The Humiliated and Abused*, labels "mystical horror"—a morbid dread of something one does not know what. Indeed, the beginning chapters of that novel are a catalog of Dostoevsky's devices of argument and inversion, whether in the opening two sentences—"Last year on the evening of March twenty-second the strangest thing happened to me. I had spent the whole day walking around town looking for an apartment"—or in a few paragraphs near the end of part 1, chapter 10, paragraphs in which the dialogue is banal and repetitive, connections between the characters are only inferred, and the space each character occupies is a projection of the other's perception:

> "Azorka's dead, too?"
>
> "Yes, Azorka's dead, too," I replied, and her question seemed odd, as if she were certain that Azorka definitely had to have died with the old man.
>
> After hearing my reply, the girl silently left the room, carefully closing the door behind her.
>
> A minute later, I ran out after her, filled with regret that I had let her go. She had left so quietly that I hadn't heard her open the other door onto the stairs. She couldn't yet have gotten downstairs—so I thought—and I stopped in the vestibule to listen. But everything was quiet, no sound of steps. Somewhere on a lower floor a door banged, and everything became quiet again.[12]

The mirror in the mirror-held-to-life is Ivan Petrovich's first novel, which he reads to his adoptive parents. With conventional middle-class taste, they respond by asking for exaltation and deploring depiction of actuality. In that sense, too, Dostoevsky completely controls the presentation. All his devices serve to make vibrant and meaningful what has previously been invisible.

He insists that he is not making something from nothing. He has his characters assert it, too. Locked in separate, unreliable partialities, they all suppose in a different space-time a harmonious whole where they would be complete. Opposite to established reality, this condition is described as "the happy summer of childhood" or "the harmony of nature" or simply "America," always representing an alluring idea of freedom. It is the positive goal believed in by all men except the self-tormentors. The dislocations of fiction expose what lies under the manicured surface of social life.

Throughout Dostoevsky's work there are frequent references to the Gospels, to Lazarus's and Jesus' resurrections, to visions of Paradise, but the difficult dilemma that Dostoevsky became ever more skilled at solving was establishing through language a coherent system depicting actuality and a deviant, ideal, revolutionary form of life most explicitly represented by Zosima, "the Russian monk." Functioning as a partial man is not enough; one's nature demands that one be complete.

If Dostoevsky had been a philosopher, he might have begun by demonstrating the rational coherence of his assumptions, as Plato begins the *Phaedrus* by declaring that "all soul is immortal," that if "that which moves itself is precisely identifiable with soul, it must follow that soul is not born and does not die." Or as Aristotle begins the *Metaphysics:* "All men naturally desire knowledge." After an historical survey, he asserts that "it is obvious there is some first principle."

Whatever Dostoevsky believes, he makes no logical assumptions, and he imposes no rational scheme. Although he may agree with Aristotle that the wise man regenerates theoretical understanding by applying experience, he does not assume a material-spiritual dichotomy. For him, motive is not a "final cause"; often "formal cause" is mere chance. In short, he takes the world as it comes.

Antithetical to the world, asserting freedom and denying the values of established reality, is the monastery, but it is not a goal to which men should aspire, and its terms cannot be measured by society's conventional wisdom. It exists partly in the mind and partly in fact, complete in itself, untranslatable, opposite to what is. Father Zosima's final profession of faith says so.

The narrator of *The Karamazov Brothers,* a resident of the same district as the Karamazovs, swings 180 degrees away from his portrait of old Fyodor after a supper of dishwater soup and overdone chicken lustfully awaiting Grushenka to a description of Alyosha's visit to the dying Zosima and of Alyosha's composite narrative "From the Sacred Life of the Late Reverend Elder Father Zosima, Compiled from His Own Words by Aleksei Fyodorovich Karamazov." The digression is double-framed. First, as Zosima, intervening in the struggle between old Fyodor and son Dmitry, had bowed low before Dmitry, and Alyosha, coming to see Zosima for the last time, had bowed before him, so Zosima, his hand to his heart in pain, surrounded by worshipers, "still smiling at them, peacefully slipped from his chair to the floor onto his knees, then bowed his head to the ground, spread his arms and, as if in joyful ecstasy, kissing the earth and praying (as he himself had taught) peacefully and joyfully surrendered his soul to God."[13] Second, as Grushenka is the object of desire for both Fyodor and Dmitry, so, after Zosima's death, disillusioned by the stench and the absence of miracle,

Alyosha goes to her in his quest for self-destruction, and she, in turn, confesses her baseness and asks for love and forgiveness. Rakitin, Alyosha's pseudo-alter ego, a false seminarian who wrote a pamphlet on Zosima and who wants to marry Khokhlakova for her money, led him there in exchange for a promised twenty-five rubles.

The maudlin, complex plotting not only emphasizes the force of the chaos opposing any one person's efforts to control his life but also presents an actual mediocrity against which to pit understanding and skill. Money, for example, an emblem of corruption, is repeatedly used by one person to buy another and, by coincidence, to seem to supply motives for various acts, the assumption being that everyone wants it. The challenge for Dostoevsky is not to idealize the pure-in-heart, who abjure it, but to supply them other, credible motives and to make the alternative they envision no less real than actuality, to create an artistic picture adequately embracing the incoherence of daily life and the systematic skepticism of reason.

He conceives character organically, each being measured by its own proportions, or from the inside out, idiosyncratically. He accepts prevailing social conventions but supposes that, like speech, all manners conceal as much as they express. He begins anywhere, acknowledging the facts: "Aleksei Fyodorovich Karamazov was the third son of a landowner in our district, Fyodor Pavlovich Karamazov . . . " Then he shifts to a focus on the bizarre, thereby creating suspense—". . . celebrated in his time (and still remembered in ours) for his tragic and mysterious end exactly thirteen years ago, which I will come to."[14] The literariness of the narrative dominates—almost imperceptibly dominates—the frenzied actions. Even Karamazov the old debaucher, called an "eccentric type," is immediately pinned by a contradiction that delimits his character and advances the plot: "Fyodor Pavlovich began practically with nothing, was the very smallest landowner, ran around dining at others' houses, wormed his way in as a hanger-on, but at the time of his death it turned out that he had some hundred thousand rubles in cash."[15]

Dostoevsky's ventriloquism is deft and captivating: The narrator sets up Alyosha as a transparent scribe for splicing Zosima's conversations into a life story quite different from the standard saint's life (such as "Aleksei, Man of God" in the medieval *Chetyi-minei*). For one thing, Zosima tells his story in the first person not as a parable but, like Augustine, as a confession. Scriptural texts and hagiographies he regards as useful for Orthodox Christians, but the force impelling a man to a meaningful life comes from within, he asserts. One may be guided by another, as he, the elder, would guide Alyosha, but no man lives another's life. Part of the authority for his position comes from the several levels of diction he uses, moving into Church Slavonic constructions when seeking illustrative parallels, expressing himself colloquially when giving his history as an army officer.

Dostoevsky so projects the tone and vocabulary of his distinct characters that we accept their existence and their roles regardless of their banality. We are constantly engaged with them in their attempts at self-expression, even as Zosima tries to redefine his adjectives: "We almost took pride in getting drunk, debauched and showing off. I wouldn't say we were basically bad; all those young men were sound, but we behaved badly, and worst of all I."[16]

The characters' fundamental intelligence and insecurity prevent such introspection from becoming intolerably sentimental, although Dostoevsky repeatedly presses to the edge. Knowing too much to continue behaving as he has, Zosima sees that he is absurd but does not know what to do except to repudiate his next step. The courage to accept his own grotesqueness endears him to us. Finding the girl he thought he could marry suddenly married to another, Zosima provokes a duel; on the eve of the duel, he wakes in the night:

> And suddenly I understood what was wrong: that I had struck Afanasy yesterday! I saw the whole thing again, as if it were happening all over—he's standing in front of me, and I hit him hard right across the face, and he keeps standing at attention, head high, eyes fixed as on parade, shudders at each blow and doesn't dare even raise his hand to ward it off—that's what a man has come to, that's a man beating a man! What criminality! Like a sharp needle going through my very soul. I stand there stunned, while the gentle sun is shining, the little leaves are cheerful, shimmering, and the birds, all the birds of the air are praising God—I covered my face with both hands, fell on my bed and sobbed. And then I remembered my brother Markel and what he said to the servants before he died: "Beloved, dear ones, why do you serve me, why do you love me, indeed am I worthy of being served by you?" "Indeed, am I worthy?" popped into my head. . . . And suddenly I realized the whole truth, saw the whole thing clearly: What was I about to do? I was about to kill a kind, intelligent, noble man in no way at fault, depriving his bride of her happiness forever, tormenting her and killing her. . . . And I ran back to the apartment alone, straight to Afanasy's little room: "Afanasy," I say to him, "yesterday I struck you in the face twice; forgive me!" I say that. He shudders as if scared, looks up, and I see that saying that is nothing, nothing, and so, just as I am, epaulettes and all, I bow down to the ground, to his feet—"Forgive me!" I say. He's stupefied. "Your honor, *batyushka,* sir, how could you . . . indeed, am I worthy?" And he began crying as I had, covered his face with both hands and turned to the window.[17]

The imaginative projection by which Zosima discovered another man and his suffering allows us to enter his story. The sequence of repeated phrases and mimetic acts, imitative of oral narrative, establishes a pattern of relations. The recurrent gesture of bowing low offers visual clarity and intellectual ambiguity in an unconventional sense, hinting at some secret force that compels master and man for a mystifying moment to sense themselves as one and to appear to the reader as equally human, repeating the gesture, repeating the words. If such moments are the most "real," the elements of reality, then we can see how brightly the convent, the most plausible community of men in such moments, served Dostoevsky as a means for experimenting, discovering, and judging.

Zosima advises mildly and modestly, knowing that other people's limits of understanding are more conventional than his, as his fellow regimental officers could understand his not firing in the duel only in the light of his resigning his commission and becoming a monk. Conventionality masks isolation; isolation breeds infidelity. He who is most isolated is most corrupt in two senses: Misunderstood, misunderstanding, a bastard and a gargoyle of a thinker, Smerdyakov murders his father; zealously pursuing a rational scheme of cause and effect and insisting that what cannot be defined does not exist (for example, God), Ivan implicates himself in the murder and comes to his own diabolism. Like Zosima, he beats a peasant and repents; like Mikhail, he confesses and is not believed. Unable to contain his own contradictions, he goes mad. The total exaggeration that is the novel is made credible by each event's, each act's being cemented in place to form an arch of characters. Zosima is the keystone.

Zosima's function occurs in condensed form in the story he tells about Mikhail, a well-to-do social benefactor of fifty, with a young wife and three small children, who called on Zosima one evening after Zosima had submitted his resignation and moved to another apartment. What had Zosima felt at the duel, Mikhail hesitantly inquired, when, instead of firing back at his opponent, he begged forgiveness? Zosima recounted the episode with Afanasy. Mikhail began to call on him more often. "Life is paradise," Mikhail said one day. "I've thought about that a lot. . . . It's all I think about." Later, he added, "Paradise is concealed in each of us. . . . And each one is guilty for all and for everything, in addition to his own sins, you were absolutely right about that. Amazing how you suddenly so completely grasped that idea. In very deed, it's true that once people understand that idea, the kingdom of Heaven will become real for them, not in dream but in fact."[18]

Young Zosima's office is imperceptibly to extract his own ideas from what the older Mikhail says. Mikhail talks, but Zosima relays the conversations to Alyosha, and Alyosha, as he writes them down, attributes them to Zosima. Zosima's skeptical responses provoke Mikhail's assertion of chiliastic faith and, finally, his confession.

Mikhail begins by saying that neither science nor the sense of a common interest will ever enable men to share property and rights without harming each other. The kingdom of Heaven will come only at the end of the era of "human separateness," the dominant characteristic of their time, he says, in which each man wants to experience the fullness of life in himself although he in fact experiences perfect suicide. Instead of reaching the fullness of the definition of being, he falls into complete isolation: "Everyone isolates himself in his own hole, everyone cuts himself off from others, hides himself and what he has, and ends up pulling away from people and driving people away from himself. . . . He becomes used to relying on himself alone."

As public interest in Zosima's scandal wanes and as Mikhail's secret presses, Mikhail and Zosima draw closer. One day Mikhail bursts out, "I killed someone."

Alone of the great nineteenth-century Russian writers, Dostoevsky wrote nothing for the theater. Perhaps he did not because the contradictions that his characters express are controlled and shaped by his auctorial interpolations. Whoever adapts a Dostoevsky fiction to stage or film reduces it to its visual aspects, eliminating the tension between feeling and idea, that delicate balance in which the quintessential artistry lies. For example, Zosima's response to Mikhail's admission: "Even as he said it he smiled, he himself as white as chalk. 'Why is he smiling?' The notion shot through me before I could make sense of anything. I myself paled." Zosima then summarizes Mikhail's story of murdering the girl he loved who turned him down and framing her manservant Pyotr. Arrested, Pyotr died of fever shortly after his trial began. Mikhail might have seemed home free, but as Zosima puts it, "With that his punishment began."[19]

For three years Mikhail has been longing to confess to his wife, although he fears that he will thereby jeopardize his children's future. Zosima's withdrawal from the duel has given him determination—"Looking at you, I reproached myself and envied you." "But they won't believe you," Zosima says, "it's been fourteen years." He prays; Mikhail anguishes; then Zosima declares that Mikhail should tell everyone, that everything passes, that only truth remains, and that whatever he does magnanimously his children will later understand. Mikhail dashes off, unexpectedly reappears at midnight, says he forgot something, then that he hasn't, that he just wanted to sit down for a moment. He makes Zosima sit down, too. Zosima reports, "We sat there a couple of minutes, he looking intently at me, and then he suddenly laughed—I remember that—then got up, fondly embraced me and kissed me. 'Remember,' he says, 'how I came to you twice. You hear—remember that!' "

Mikhail does confess, but in fact, although he announces it in public at his own birthday party, nobody believes him. He soon falls ill, is about to die with his secret. After several attempts, Zosima gets in to see him and comforts him a last time: "He managed to whisper to me: 'Remember how I came to your place a second time at midnight? and told you to be sure to remember? You know why I came? I came to kill you!' "[20]

Certainly the plotting is melodramatic—Dostoevsky leads his characters up to one brink after another—but the tension transforms it into significant gesture. Embodied in language, it will not translate into another form. Dostoevsky conceived characters in their separatenesses, accurately reflecting actual social experience, but projected them in dramatic reciprocity through language. Each character's response depends on another's feeling, linking motive to projected symbol. For example, when Mikhail comes back at midnight, he addresses Zosima not in the second person plural *vy* but in the second singular *ty*: "For the first time he said *ty* to me. And left. 'Tomorrow,' thought I."

How crucially definitive that is, is suggested to us by Anna's reflection in *Anna Karenina* that, as she becomes estranged from her husband, she must speak only French to him to use the cool but respectful *vous,* for she cannot bear the intimacy of the Russian *ty*, and after years of marriage *vy* is unspeakable. Mikhail's use of *ty* identifies an intense intimacy for which we have been half prepared by Zosima's ability to accept human behavior, beginning with his own, as a dynamic compound of irrepressible longings.

As Mikhail repeats the phrase "Remember I came a second time" with its Gospel echoes, he aesthetically completes the gesture. The motive he confesses is not the one that Zosima accepts or Dostoevsky reveals. Because Mikhail did not kill Zosima, his passion is expressed purely as love. The strength, indeed the brilliance, of his passion expresses Zosima's vitality: The man who is most alive calls forth life in others. Zosima had already experienced and understood the mixed self-love and self-hate—the "guilt"—that Mikhail talked about, so that, to an exceptional degree, he not only reciprocated Mikhail's desire but also, in the aptness of his understanding, participated in everything Mikhail did. Ultimately, in his special goodness, he anticipates everything men can do, comes as close as Dostoevsky can come to representing what "the good life" means not as an abstract ideal or a purseful of superstitions but as the practical composite of a vocabulary of actions around "responsibility," "guilt," "justice," "freedom," or the very idea of "a man."

As Zosima's history shows, for a man's form of life to change, his behavior, too, must express the change. His story of it, like the anthology of stories that is the whole novel, expresses the terms by which he measures the coherence of its parts and tests its truthfulness. As if to prove the unreliability of superstitious witnesses and the shallowness of those who want miracles (a miracle is a violation of natural law), Zosima's corpse does not smell sweet and his coffin does not fly out the window.

Of course, intellectual problems remain: Can Zosima's teachings be generalized? Do the beauty and mystery of the world necessarily testify to the existence of God? Zosima's precepts are not difficult to translate, but his actions are, for they require finding simultaneously with every event the context of transcendent values that makes it meaningful. Eight years after parting from Afanasy, Zosima happens to meet him. (Only the novel can supply the terms for transforming coincidence into fate.) The two men have reversed their separate lives: Zosima is a mendicant monk; Afanasy, a street vendor, married with two small children. When they meet, they exchange positions: Having turned all his money over to his monastery when he joined it, Zosima shares the communal life. At Afanasy's place after tea, Afanasy gives him two half-rubles—one for the monastery, one for himself on his wanderings. As Afanasy has the generosity to give, so Zosima has the generosity to accept, thereby completing the gesture and, without diminishing Afanasy, taking on himself responsibility for them both: "I accepted his half-ruble, bowed to him and his wife and left overjoyed, thinking to myself on the way: 'Now the both of us, he in his place and I walking along, are oh-ing and ah-ing, probably, and laughing cheerfully in our hearts' delight, shaking our heads and thinking back how God brought us together.' I haven't seen him since. I was his master, and he, my servant, but then, as we kissed each other on the cheek fondly and with spiritual tenderness, a sense of great human unity passed between us. I've thought about it much."[21]

Why can that unity not be extended to the whole Russian people? he asks. From his point of view, there is no reason. He has, so to speak, prelived the lives of all who, like Afanasy or like us, speak the language of this book; therefore, his form of life is the ideal even though no one else can attain it.

10

The Long View

There is no absolute standard of pitch.
—*Hindemith*

UNLIKE OTHER MASTERFUL, IMAGINATIVE, and in their day more popular novelists such as Hawthorne, Dickens, Flaubert, and Tolstoy, Melville and Dostoevsky seemed to their contemporary readers iconoclastic. Melville was admired for sea adventure and South Pacific romanticism; Dostoevsky, for urban *trompe l'oeil* and action plotting. Both were too investigative, too original to be read for what they had written. Other writers caused superficial concern, indicated alternative values, created memorable characters in artistic works of great skill, but in their work did not press hard questions against the prevailing way of life.

After the trial-generated scandal around *Madame Bovary* in 1857 had passed, Emma's story remained an exquisite portrayal of the incommensurability of passion and provincial life. We readers acknowledge her bravery in her self-defeat and agree that she had no place to go. As Flaubert commented in the novel, "Elle retrouvait dans l'adultère toutes les platitudes du mariage." *Anna Karenina* is a novel of scope, sensibility, and extraordinary literary excellence; Levin's way of life stands as a moral alternative to Anna's way to death, but Levin, homilist and paternalist, supports an effete social structure, a dream world of happy social bonding in which middle-class readers still want to believe. We find such affirmation of everyday life in *Sketches by Boz* and *The*

Pickwick Papers, the acceptance of suffering and a belief in Santa Claus–like recovery in *Nicholas Nickleby,* a popular success as fiction in the 1830s and a huge success as musical comedy in the 1980s chiefly because it ends with Nicholas becoming a rich and prosperous merchant, settling into his father's old house close to his sister Kate, doing nothing and nothing ever being changed. Dickens "succeeded in attacking everybody and antagonizing nobody," said George Orwell. "His criticism of society is almost exclusively moral. Hence the utter lack of any constructive suggestion anywhere in his work. . . . [His] attitude . . . is part of the English puritan tradition. . . . In his own age and ours he has been popular chiefly because he was able to express in a comic, simplified and therefore memorable form the native decency of the common man."[1]

In essays and letters, Tolstoy, too, argued for social reform, but his fiction was either tendentious, like *Resurrection* or "After the Ball," or a projection of individual conflicts that did not disturb the status quo. Like Dickens, writing in the 1850s and 1860s, he built idealized landscapes through a child's acute perceptions or through his own romanticization of the early years of the century. For all its scope, range of experience, philosophizing, and multitude of characters, *War and Peace* is an historical novel.

The Marble Faun is a romance, and most of Hawthorne's work deals with what he called "the truth of the human heart," the power of blackness in human nature that cries out for confession. Secret sin, the source of suffering, leads men to wisdom, although the framework for the fictions is that austere Puritanism whose values of self-denial and divine inscrutability were part of the prevalent Protestant ethic. Flaubert's novel about the political events of 1848, *A Senti-*

mental Education, stitches a simplistic triad of revolutionary points of view onto a middle-class love story.

In castigating social embrace of technology and materialism, in attacking industrial culture for emptiness, and revolutionary change for merely foreshadowing disillusion, Dostoevsky and Melville were a generation or two ahead of themselves. Melville died unnoticed and almost unremembered. Ironically, all literate Russia read *The Karamazov Brothers* as it appeared serially, and in those last years of his life, Dostoevsky, once a political prisoner, was a frequent if somewhat lugubrious guest in the highest circles of Petersburg church and court society.

Another way to report that is to say that Melville was *un*read and Dostoevsky was *mis*read. In the dominant atmosphere of piety and naturalism, they were read straight, as if they were illustrators, not illusionists whose firm minds were building meaning through structural patterns and the rhythms of prose. Their fictional characters were mistaken for real people instead of the coordinated, or rhythmic, replacements in consciousness that they are. And the landscapes they inhabited were thought to be representational instead of ersatz spaces adapted from ordinary life and made four-dimensional by the addition of all the time in the characters' lives.

Every successful work of art is aesthetically a complete, self-referential unity, a little finite, unbounded universe. Extraordinarily, Dostoevsky and Melville made that universe synonymous with the power of generative consciousness: The substance of the mind is the story, whether expressed as Ahab's quest or Ivan Karamazov's poem. The work of art *is* a transformation of life, from an ordinary point of view making nothing out of something—turning the material into the immaterial—but from the viewpoint of the central consciousness perfecting the universe.

For most people, life passes in unmolested routine. Their actions and thoughts are habitual, irregularly interrupted by accidents, changes of weather, rewards, losses, and coincidences. Accustomed to miles of road, they move along mechanically, often unable afterward to recall what they have seen or to explain why they are where they are. For all they know, it is as if they never moved. The first half of Melville's "Field Asters" says this:

> Like the stars in commons blue
> Peep their namesakes, Asters here,
> Wild ones every autumn seen—
> Seen of all, arresting few.

The writer's eye arrests ordinary objects in their distinctive separatenesses, distancing them from us into significant details. The significance comes from unexpected but universal reciprocity:

> Seen indeed. But who their cheer
> Interpret may, or what they mean
> When so inscrutably their eyes
> Us star-gazers scrutinize.[2]

Both Dostoevsky and Melville believed that the world was formed in love and that the attributes of any part were predicated on the existence of an other. This concept of mutuality beyond the seesaw and the reciprocating engine asserts that the existence of one figure determines the qualities of the other, as Adam's sonship is established by God's existence, and God's fatherhood, by Adam's existence. Because each thing exists finally in terms of everything else, the artist's task is to establish the context that makes the relations intelligible—or paraphrasing Glinka, Dostoevsky's favorite composer, as quoted in chapter 8, the artist must harmonize a world of experience while preserving melodic individuality.

In late twentieth-century terms, we might think of it as the need to find a unified field theory, the drive toward which comes from the power of mystery. In an 1861 article, Dostoevsky showed how, looking across the Neva into the heart of St. Petersburg one cold January evening, he discovered the organic, autonomous, palingenetic life of the mind:

It seemed, finally, that this whole world, with all its inhabitants strong and weak, with all their dwellings, the hovels of the poor and the gilded palaces, in this evening hour was like a fantastic, magical vision, a dream, which in turn will immediately vanish and rise like steam in the dark blue sky. A strange idea suddenly stirred inside me. I shuddered, and my heart in that moment seemed flooded by a hot stream of blood, suddenly boiling up in the onrush of a mighty but previously unknown sensation. In that instant, I seemed to have understood something that until then had merely stirred in me unintelligibly, to have perceived something new, some absolutely new world, unfamiliar to me and known only from some vague rumors, from some mysterious signs. I think that it was precisely in those moments that my existence begin.[3]

In awe of such mystery and out of respect for the historical church and its god, and hoping to restore his faith, Melville visited the Holy Land four years before the Civil War. For the next twenty years he worked on a long poem, *Clarel,* projecting his inquiry for a standard of moral judgment. He concluded that there was no new revelation and no salvation, only heroic struggle and lonely sorrow. At best, Christ's building mansions in Heaven had made it impossible for men to be "content with life's own discontent."[4]

Young Clarel, a modern Magus seeking the place of Jesus' birth and the experiences and understanding that attend a successful quest, becomes too aware of tragedy to accept a Messiah. "Grief is the chamberlain to knowledge," said the narrator of *Pierre*; in *Clarel* this is expanded into a psychology of suffering.[5] In summarizing all the book-length critical studies of *Clarel*, Vincent Kenny showed the metaphysical and vast cultural dimensions in which Melville cast his almost unreadable poem.[6] The squib that he scribbled in his copy of *Don Quixote* applies to himself and to his various self-projections—"A god-like mind without a God"—nowhere more conspicuously than in the long poem. He had not written himself into a corner, but he had written without readers or constituents. In an earlier age, *Clarel* would have been a morality play, for it required an audience with a communal sensibility.

On his quest for Christ's birthplace and the Rose of Sharon, caught in moribund Jerusalem encircled by Turks, Clarel visits the actual sites of Christ's life and imagines himself back into Christ's time—the only time that Jerusalem was alive—then into Allah's, into Buddha's, into Brahma's. A mad evangelist named Nehemiah serves him as a kind of Virgil and substitute Christ. Clarel falls in love with Ruth, daughter of Agar, who dreams of America as a new Eden, and of a Jewish Illinois farmer named Nathan, whom marauding Arabs kill. Ruth's seclusion for mourning leaves Clarel free to go on a pilgrimage with Vine, a recluse, and Rolfe, a vigorous inquirer.

Going through the Wilderness, Clarel meets Mortmain, a black-clothed utopist disillusioned by the events of 1848, and a Syrian monk living "out his life in expiation, knowing that the ambiguities will never be solved in life."[7] On the third day by the Dead Sea, a vision of the Southern Cross expresses the barrenness of modern Christianity. Mortmain returns from a night-long vigil obsessed with omnipresent sin and evil, and Nehemiah, believing that God has called him to the New Jerusalem, walks into the Dead Sea. In the morning Vine discovers the body.

The third part of the poem takes place at "Mar Saba," a monastery in the Judah Mountains. There is singing in Greek; there is monkish chanting. Old sailor Agath spins an Ancient Mariner–like tale of suffering and loss aboard the ship *The Peace of God.* Then follows a long discussion on hypocrisy and the study of a little palm tree on a ledge—What does it symbolize? On the seventh morning, Clarel finds Mortmain dead, an eagle feather on his lips.

As they cross the desert to Bethlehem, the pilgrims are heavy with the sense of tragedy. Ungar, a military Southerner, joins the group. They spend a night in the Capuchin monastery of the Church of the Nativity and review the Christianity of the Middle Ages. On the ninth night, a Frenchman shares Clarel's room, praises the voluptuousness of Jewish women. And on the following day, Ash Wednesday, back in Jerusalem, they pass the cemetery where Agar, dead from fever, and Ruth, dead from grief, are being buried. Soon left alone, Clarel goes through the rites of Holy Week. On the feast of Pentecost, he sets out with a new group of pilgrims along the Via Dolorosa on what must be an endless quest for an unattainable faith.

How conscious and controlled can poetry be? How accessible can it be made? "How much poetry will be left when we finish?" Randall Jarrell asked. "Auden's [answer] . . . is too conscious, too thin, too merely rational: we should distrust it just as we distrust any Rational (or Rationalized) Method of Becoming a Saint."[8] If you find Auden's *Age of Anxiety* much less than an extraordinary achievement and more a projection of Auden's own anxiety, guilt, and isolation than a significant social statement, you should not be surprised by the discrepancy between intellectual earnestness and technical accomplishment in *Clarel.* After reading the poem, you may be tempted to repeat what the *Atlantic Monthly*'s reviewer said about *Battle-Pieces:* "[It shows] negative virtues of originality in such degree that it not only reminds you of no poetry you have read but of no life you have known."[9]

I think Melville's poem presents a Hans Castorp in the 1870s. In *The Magic Mountain,* Castorp goes on two quests—one, for health, to the sanitorium; the other, for definition, to Naphta (Left) and Settembrini (Right). Both quests assume physical solutions. In *Clarel,* the young man in search of spiritual health goes to the Holy Land to the physical, monastic sources of what he wishes were a plausible faith. Like Castorp, he assumes that mind and body are well or ill together, that each is an expression of the other—as if by being in the *right* place one would be in one's right mind. From that it seems but a small step to the concept that one's proper legacy is moral rightness—right reason and faith combine.

The idea is not new, but each assertion of it must be made against—or in spite of—man's skeptical bias on behalf of practical morality. If for a moment we set aside our materialism and our shibboleth "progress," perhaps we can see that more than genes is passed on from generation to generation. Speaking of exogenetic, or cultural, evolution as well as genetic, or biological, Thomas Morgan said, "There are, then, in man two processes of inheritance: one through the physical continuity of the germ-cells; and the other through the transmission of the experiences of one generation to the next by means of example and by spoken and written language. . . . In the human race, . . . a prolonged period of childhood furnishes exceptional opportunities for the transmission of tradition and experience."[10]

On the day after his first wife's death, Dostoevsky reflected in his notebook on the consequences of the spiritual following from the physical and vice versa:

> Man, as he physically engenders a son, transmits to him a part of his own personal individuality, and thus morally leaves a memory of himself to people . . . that is, he introduces a part of his former earthly personality into the future development of mankind. . . . Christ entered entirely into humanity, and man strives to transform himself into the *I* of Christ or into his own ideal. . . . A man on earth strives toward an ideal *opposed* to his nature. . . . Man must constantly experience suffering, which is offset by the heavenly delight of fulfilling the Law, that is, sacrificing. In this lies earthly equilibrium.[11]

Dostoevsky's passion eluded Melville. *Clarel* is his most intense study in the causes and condition of a skepticism based on the assumption that faith is possible. But his suffering is not offset by any heavenly delight; from Christ's suffering he derives the passive, necessary wisdom of patience, by which a man carries on. He shows, as J. G. Knapp commented, that "only in endurance will man prevail."[12]

Between *Clarel* and *The Magic Mountain* came World War I, which gravely weakened the ideal of democratic, or reform, liberalism and destroyed the community of belief, the community to which Dostoevsky looked when, forty years earlier, he jotted in his notebook for *The Karamazov Brothers*, "I say that if the church, the whole church replaced the state, then there would be no injustice."[13] In the strength of his faith, his tenets were practical and angels were real. As the novel was being serialized in June 1879, he wrote the assistant editor, "If I'm successful, I'll achieve something very fine: *compelling the reader to admit* that a pure, ideal Christian isn't an abstraction but graphically real, plausible, clearly imminent."[14]

Despite the harsh treatment they received in prison or on ship and despite the wars they lived through, neither Dostoevsky nor Melville anticipated the pervasive spiritual destruction caused by the dehumanizing trench warfare of 1914–18 and the inhuman labor camps, gas chambers, mass air raids, and nuclear war of 1934–45. Melville wondered,

Over and over, again and again
Must the fight for the Right be fought?[15]

not supposing that half a century after his death, as Americans were reading his work with pleasure and respect, the answer would be, "it makes no difference," and that a couple of tramps, waiting for Godot, would disinterestedly philosophize in the desert.

Sometimes, I suppose Dostoevsky was relieved at not having to live by his own declarations or to adapt his idiosyncrasies like the uncle in Melville's story "The Happy Failure." After ten years' labor, Uncle finds that his hydraulic-hydrostatic invention does not work. His black servant Yorpy says, "Yoo is yourself agin in de ten long 'ear," and Uncle, relieved of pursuing his monomania, cries, "Praise be to God for the failure!"[16] Both Dostoevsky and Melville were tormented by the temptations of intellectual opposites, by the sadomasochism of proud passion, and by the gross inequalities of fortune. "The rich in their craving glut, as the poor in their craving want, we have with us always," says the narrator in Melville's "Jimmy Rose," and in another sketch he begs, "Heaven save me equally from the 'Poor Man's Pudding' and the 'Rich Man's Crumbs.' "[17]

Individual men are aware of civilized society's continual failure to make the means of production respond to universal social needs, but Walter Benjamin says that men are aware collectively, also. Driven by pain and by ambition to strive for social change, they do not trust what they might achieve for fear of losing what they have. They repudiate their fathers' failures in the name of an idealized past, which they have projected onto an invisible future. In fact, he says, monuments of art are the unique signs of that utopia:

> Corresponding in the collective consciousness to the forms of the new means of production, which at first were still dominated by the old (Marx), are images in which the new is intermingled with the old. These images are wishful fantasies, and in them the collective seeks both to preserve and to transfigure the inchoateness of the social product and the deficiencies in the social system of production. . . . These tendencies direct the visual imagination, which has been activated by the new, back to the primeval past. In the dream in which, before the eyes of each epoch, that which is to follow appears in images, the latter appears wedded to elements from prehistory, that is, of a classless society. Intimations of this, deposited in the unconscious of the collective, mingle with the new to produce the utopia that has left its traces in thousands of configurations of life, from permanent buildings to fleeting fashions.[18]

Perhaps one cannot come closer than that to defining the social cause of artistic production or the relation between material provocation and mode of response. Given things as they are—putrefaction of both the whale's body and the monk's as the ultimate actuality—we can say only that some men make their way, others do not. In *Netochka Nezvanova,* we follow several ordinary violinists; in "The Fiddler," we come on the extraordinary, an artist *with* genius and *without* fame who wants no more than he has. Perfectly adjusted to art and to life, Hautboy always makes the apt, aesthetically elegant response, but he expresses understanding of forms, not of dilemmas of good and evil.

Like Benjamin's distanced criticism, Hautboy's cool, imitable perfection is an aspect of art seen from outside an artist's consciousness. From inside, the view is much different, as Dostoevsky's and Melville's letters remind us. In 1960, Boris Pasternak in a letter written in English to an English translator stated some of the differences with poignant simplicity:

> From the beginning I have been absorbed by the great, earnest, vivid, essential. It took place in an old developed traditional society with its richly ramified familiar manners, tastes and forms. The tastes of the time as well as our young boyish attempts were allowed to go astray in the forest of smallest and darkest particularities and details. Those oddities were not incomprehensible then. They were bone of the bone[,] flesh of the flesh of the date. The time recognized itself in these singularities. But they could not exist independently. They could not be transferred out of that period and that society in[to] some other sphere. I think they had not the least value out of this surrounding. Not only the substance of the strange arts of the time,—far more, their contents lay in the life of the age. The *sense* of the poetry, and all the creative expression of the period has been furnished and supported by how it was custom to live, to err, to hope, to see, to think, to suffer in those years.[19]

Can the world improve? Is it, as Evert Duyckinck comments on Melville's view of the *Neversink,* really a "frigate with its thousand picked men, the contribution of every state of life, of every stage of civilization, of each profession, of all arts and callings," an all-male world "divorced from humanity itself"?[20] In practical, political terms, will heaven always be some kind of "Paradise of Bachelors"?

Dostoevsky said that it was not. He believed that an

unreformed, drunk Russian peasant contained the potential for his own transformation, that he might say with Melville's narrator in "The Lightning-Rod Man," "In thunder as in sunshine, I stand at ease in the hands of my God . . . and in the blue heavens I read in the rainbow, that the Deity will not, of purpose, make war on man's earth."[21] The calmness of a brighter region is dreamed of by "Benito Cereno's" Captain Delano, also, who does not understand the nature of evil but who envisions the monastery as the perfect ship, the world in which talent and justice are balanced. Charles Nicol noted that

> the monastery is after all one type of the paradise of bachelors: a strictly male society where all work in fellowship for a common good. It is not surprising then that the *San Dominick* (Melville named the ship for the founder of one of the monastic orders) is first seen as a white monastery full of Black Friars (Dominicans), that the name *Benito* is Spanish for Benedictine monk, that Cereno is described as "like some hypochondriac abbot" and Babo as "like a begging friar of St. Francis." This, Melville suggests, is the type of social order ideally seen aboard ship, the one dreamed of by innocent Delano, though doubtless few ships even remotely approach such an ideal community of fellowship and shared will.[22]

To Dostoevsky and Melville, the apparent social harmonies and moral order of the eighteenth century were illusory. To recapture the values of reason and fairness despite the losses of the Civil War and the Russo-Turkish War and the even politically incomplete manumission of the serfs and freeing of the slaves, they turned to the stars to get a measure on man, whom they saw physically swelling but spiritually shrinking in the ever-accelerating process of industrialization.

They themselves were not monks, although from time to time in their lives they lived like monks, and all their lives they imagined what men by their nature could be. They saw that a declaration of self-evident truths was political fustian. They knew that words, like men, turn over and must be turned over again. Leaning forward, looking backward, driven by an inner, cacophonous iconoclasm, they found how to measure the worst by the best in the worlds around them, how to laugh at the ironies and other irreducible denominators, and how to bequeath to a couple of generations after them a still-living tradition.

Notes

Chapter 1

1. J. A. N. C. de Condorcet, *Esquisse d'un tableau historique des progrès de l'esprit humain* (Paris: Editions Boivin, 1933), p. 210.

2. John Locke, *Treatise of Civil Government* and *A Letter Concerning Toleration* (New York: Appleton-Century-Crofts, 1937), pp. 5, 14–15, 217.

3. Joseph Warton, "Ode I. To Fancy," in *Eighteenth Century Poetry and Prose,* ed. Louis Bredvold, Alan McKillop, and Lois Whitney (New York: Ronald Press, 1939), p. 565 (lines 113–20).

4. Laurence Sterne, Letter to Mr. and Mrs. James, November 12, 1767, in *A Sentimental Journey through France and Italy with Selections from the Journals, Sermons and Correspondence,* ed. W. L. Cross (New York: Liveright, 1926), p. 283.

5. Jean-Jacques Rousseau, *The Social Contract,* trans. Maurice Cranston (Harmondsworth: Penguin, 1968), pp. 135, 149.

6. Walter Armstrong, *Sir Joshua Reynolds* (New York: Charles Scribner's Sons, 1905), facsimile insert following p. 226.

7. *The Poetical Works of Alexander Pope,* ed. John Hogben (London: M. Walter Scott, 1887), p. 137 (Book 1, lines 45–72). "Jacob" refers to Jacob Tonson, bookseller.

8. Homer *Odyssey,* trans. Robert Fitzgerald (New York: Doubleday Anchor, 1963), p. 114.

9. William Wordsworth, "The Prelude," in *Selected Poetry,* ed. Mark Van Doren (New York: Modern Library, 1950), pp. 202–3 (Book 2, lines 233–61).

10. Charles Baudelaire, "Le crepuscule du soir," from "Tableaux parisiens," in *Les fleurs du mal* (Paris: Aux quais de Paris, n.d.), p. 111.

11. Wordsworth, "The Prelude," in *Selected Poetry,* p. 281 (Book 7, lines 149–50).

12. Ibid., p. 311 (Book 8, lines 476–94).

13. Wordsworth, "Preface to the 2nd Edition of *The Lyrical Ballads,*" in *Selected Poetry,* pp. 689–90, 693.

14. Wallace Stevens, "The Man with the Blue Guitar," in *The Collected Poems of Wallace Stevens* (New York: Knopf, 1961), pp. 166–67.

15. William B. Dillingham, *Melville's Short Fiction 1853–1856* (Athens: Univ. of Georgia Press, 1977), p. 348.

16. Antonio Gramsci, *Selections from the Prison Notebooks of Antonio Gramsci*, ed. Quintin Hoare and Geoffrey Nowell Smith (New York: International Publishers, 1977), pp. 11, 191, 214ff., 343.

17. See *The New York Review of Books*, April 30, 1981, p. 9.

18. See Otto Rank, *Truth and Reality*, trans. Jessie Taft (New York: W. W. Norton, 1978), passim.

19. Herman Melville, "Madam Mirror," in *The Collected Poems of Herman Melville*, ed. H. P. Vincent (Chicago: Packard & Co., Hendricks House, 1947), p. 371.

20. James E. Miller, Jr., *A Reader's Guide to Herman Melville* (New York: Farrar, Straus & Cudahy, 1962), p. 4. Miller calls the account "if not incorrect, at least misleading."

21. "The part self-observation may have played in the conception of the Double type is suggested in a letter that Dostoevsky wrote to a female correspondent who sought his advice on her dual impulses which, she feared, led her to commit reprehensible acts. He answered: 'That trait is common to all . . . that is, all who are not wholly commonplace. . . . It is precisely on this ground that I cannot but regard you as a twin soul, for your inner duality corresponds exactly to my own. It causes at once great torment and great delight.'

"This is a key statement in support of Dostoevsky's complete awareness of what he was about in the artistic creation of those famous characters that fall into the category of the Double. And belief in Christ, as he told his correspondent, was also his solution, however unconvincing, for the resolution of their tormenting dualism." (Ernest J. Simmons, *Introduction to Russian Realism* [Bloomington: Indiana Univ. Press, 1965], pp. 113–14)

22. Miller, *Guide to Melville*, p. 5.

23. Simmons, *Russian Realism*, pp. 109, 104.

24. R. L. Stevenson, "A Note on Realism," *The Magazine of Art* 7 (1884): 27.

25. J. V. Cunningham, *The Problem of Style* (Greenwich: Fawcett, 1966), p. 278.

26. L. P. Grossman, "Dostoevskij-xudožnik," in *Tvorčestvo F. M. Dostoevskogo*, ed. N. L. Stepanov et al. (Moscow: AN SSSR, 1959), p. 353.

27. Werner Berthoff, *The Example of Melville* (Princeton: Princeton Univ. Press, 1962), p. 140.

28. R. P. Blackmur, "The Craft of Herman Melville," in *The Expense of Greatness* (New York: Arrow, 1940), p. 148.

Chapter 2

1. Eric Auerbach, *Mimesis*, trans. Willard Trask (New York: Doubleday Anchor, 1957), p. 490.

2. Frederick Engels, *Selected Works*, trans. anon. (Moscow: Foreign Languages, 1951), 2:369.

3. Samuel Eliot Morison and Henry Steele Commager, *The Growth of the American Republic* (New York: Oxford Univ. Press, 1942), 2:136 and passim. See also Charles A. Beard and Mary R. Beard, *A Basic History of the United States* (New York: New Home Library, 1944), especially chapter 13, "The Industrial Revolution."

4. Alexis de Tocqueville, *Democracy in America*, ed. Phillips Bradley, trans. Henry Reeve (New York: Vintage Books, n.d.), 1:260–62.

5. Henry Thoreau, "Resistance to Civil Government," in *American Issues*, ed. Thorp, Curti, and Baker (Philadelphia: J. B. Lippincott, 1944), 1:498.

6. F. M. Dostoevskij, "Mal'čik u Xrista na ëlke," in *Polnoe sobranie xudožestvennyx proizvedenij*, ed. B. Tomaševskij and K. Xalabaev (Moscow and Leningrad: Gosizdat, 1926–30), 12:154–56.

7. See Jay Leyda, ed., *The Melville Log: A Documentary Life of Herman Melville, 1819–1891*, 2 vols. (New York: Harcourt, Brace, 1951), 2:640.

8. Ibid., p. 648.

9. H. Melville, "The Paradise of Bachelors and the Tartarus of Maids," in *Complete Works*, ed. Raymond Weaver (London: Constable, 1922–24), 13:228.

10. Ibid., p. 231.

11. Ibid., p. 234.

12. Ibid., pp. 242–43.

13. Ibid., pp. 245, 247.

14. George Gibian, "The Grotesque in Dostoevsky," *Modern Fiction Studies* 4, no. 3 (1958): 263ff.

15. F. M. Dostoevskij, "Čužaja žena i muž pod krovat'ju," in *Polnoe sobranie* 1:430.

16. H. Melville, *Moby-Dick,* in *Complete Works* 7:16.
17. Ibid., p. 21.
18. H. Melville, "Journal," January 1857, in *Melville Log* 2:546.
19. F. M. Dostoevskij, "Malen'kij geroj," in *Polnoe sobranie* 2:167.

Chapter 3

1. Louise Dauner, "Raskolnikov in Search of a Soul," *Modern Fiction Studies* 4, no. 3 (1958): 199.
2. Viola Sachs, *La contre-Bible de Melville:* Moby-Dick *déchiffré* (Paris and The Hague: Mouton, 1975), p. 83.
3. L. N. Tolstoj, *Vojna i mir, Polnoe sobranie sočinenij* (Moscow: N.p., 1940), 12:322–23, 329, 338.
4. H. Melville, *Mardi,* in *Complete Works,* ed. Raymond Weaver (London: Constable, 1922–24), 4:370.
5. H. Melville, "Roast Beef in the Pulpit," in *The Complete Stories of Herman Melville,* ed. Jay Leyda (London: Eyre & Spottiswoode, 1951), p. xi.
6. Ibid.
7. William B. Dillingham, *Melville's Short Fiction 1853–1856* (Athens: Univ. of Georgia Press, 1977), p. 69.
8. H. Melville, "Cock-A-Doodle-Doo!" in *Complete Stories,* p. 120.
9. Ibid., p. 121.
10. D. M. Fiene, "Bartleby the Christ," in *Studies in the Minor and Later Works of Melville,* ed. Raymona E. Hull (Hartford: Transcendental Books, 1970), p. 22.
11. F. M. Dostoevskij, *The Notebooks for* Crime and Punishment, ed. and trans. Edward Wasiolek (Chicago: Univ. of Chicago Press, 1967), pp. 69, 85, 86.
12. F. M. Dostoevskij, "Stat'i 1861 goda," in *Polnoe sobranie xudožestvennyx proizvedenij,* ed. B. Tomaševskij and K. Xalabaev (Moscow and Leningrad: Gosizdat, 1926–30), 13:86.
13. Simon Lesser, "Saint and Sinner—Dostoevsky's *Idiot,*" *Modern Fiction Studies* 4, no. 3 (1958): 211.
14. Jack Abbott, *In the Belly of the Beast* (New York: Random House, 1981), pp. 13, 74–75.
15. *The Confessions of St. Augustine,* trans. F. J. Sheed (New York: Sheed & Ward, 1942), pp. 111, 109.
16. H. Melville, "Hawthorne and His Mosses," in *Complete Works* 13:129.

17. F. M. Dostoevskij, *Dnevnik pisatelja*, in *Polnoe sobranie sočinenij v tridcati tomax*, ed. V. G. Bazanov (Leningrad: AN SSSR / Nauka, 1972–86), 26:110.

18. Anthony Hecht, "Sloth," in *The Hard Hours* (New York: Atheneum, 1967), p. 52.

19. Cf. F. M. Dostoevskij, "Stat'i 1861 goda," in *Polnoe sobranie* 13:passim.

20. Ibid., p. 86.

21. Ibid., p. 90.

22. Czeslaw Milosz, *The Captive Mind* (London: Secker & Warburg, 1953), p. 66.

23. F. M. Dostoevskij, "Ot redakcii," "Stat'i 1873 goda," in *Polnoe sobranie* 13:456.

24. F. M. Dostoevskij, *Dnevnik pisatelja*, in *Polnoe sobranie sočinenij* 26:84–86.

25. Mark 8:34–35, in the New English Bible.

26. Lev Shestov, "The Gift of Prophecy," in *Chekhov and Other Essays*, trans. anon. (Ann Arbor: Univ. of Michigan, 1966), p. 81.

27. F. M. Dostoevskij, *Brat'ja Karamazovy*, in *Sobranie sočinenij v desjati tomax*, ed. L. P. Grossman (Moscow: Goslitizdat, 1956–58), 9:138.

28. Hans Reichenbach, *Elements of Symbolic Logic* (New York: Free Press, 1947), p. 74.

29. F. M. Dostoevskij, *Zapiski iz mërtvogo doma*, in *Polnoe sobranie* 3:315.

30. *The Aeneid of Virgil* 7. 310–13, trans. C. Day Lewis (New York: Doubleday Anchor, 1953), p. 164.

31. Geza Roheim, *Psychoanalysis and Anthropology* (New York: International Universities Press, 1950), p. 473.

Chapter 4

1. H. Melville, "Hawthorne and His Mosses," in *Complete Works*, ed. Raymond Weaver (London: Constable, 1922–24), 13:138.

2. Joseph Flibbert, *Melville and the Art of Burlesque* (Amsterdam: Rodopi, 1974), pp. 32–33, 15.

3. R. P. Blackmur, "The Craft of Herman Melville," in *The Expense of Greatness* (New York: Arrow, 1940), p. 148.

4. Ibid., p. 141.

5. Gerald M. Sweeney, *Melville's Use of Classical Mythology* (Amsterdam: Rodopi, 1975), p. 56.

6. See David Jaffé, *The Stormy Petrel and the Whale: Some Origins of* Moby-Dick (Baltimore: Port City Press, 1976), passim.

7. Letters to John Murray of July 15 and September 2, 1846, in *The Letters of Herman Melville*, ed. Merrell R. Davis and William H. Gilman (New Haven: Yale Univ. Press, 1960), pp. 39, 46.

8. Ibid., p. 108.

9. H. Melville, *Redburn*, in *Complete Works* 5:326.

10. Czeslaw Milosz, *Native Realm* (New York: Doubleday, 1968), p. 138.

11. See G. M. Fridlender, "Svjatočnyj rasskaz Dostoevskogo i ballad Rjukkerta," in *Meždunarodnye svjazi russkoj literatury* (Moscow and Leningrad: Nauka, 1963), pp. 370–90.

12. Friedrich Rückert, "Des fremden Kindes heiliger Christ," in *Poetische Werke* (Frankfurt-am-Main: J. D. Sauerländer, 1868), 7:202–4.

13. Aleksandr Blok, "Svobodnaja sovest'," in *Sobranie sočinenij*, ed. K. A. Fedin et al. (Leningrad: Sovetskij pisatel', 1932–36), 10:281.

Chapter 5

1. *The Letters of Herman Melville*, ed. Merrell R. Davis and William H. Gilman (New Haven: Yale Univ. Press, 1960), p. 106.

2. From Melville's Preface to *Typee*.

3. *Neizdannye proizvedenija* N. G. *Černyševskogo* (Moscow: N.p., 1928), 3:10–12, quoted in V. V. Vinogradov, O *jazyke xudožestvennoj literatury* (Moscow: Goslitizdat, 1959), pp. 141–42.

4. M. M. Baxtin, *Problemy poètiki Dostoevskogo* (Moscow: Sovetskij pisatel', 1963), p. 92.

5. F. M. Dostoevskij, "Krotkaja," in *Polnoe sobranie xudožestvennyx proizvedenij*, ed. B. Tomaševskij and K. Xalabaev (Moscow and Leningrad: Gosizdat, 1926–30), 11:443.

6. Baxtin, *Problemy poètiki Dostoevskogo*, p. 75.

7. H. Melville, *Moby-Dick*, in *Complete Works*, ed. Raymond Weaver (London: Constable, 1922–24), 7:2.

8. Werner Berthoff, *The Example of Melville* (Princeton: Princeton Univ. Press, 1962), p. 125.

9. H. Melville, *Moby-Dick*, in *Complete Works* 7:182.

10. Ibid., p. 154.

11. Ramon Fernandez, *Messages* (Paris: Nouvelle revue française, 1926), pp. 59–62.

12. Berthoff, *Example of Melville*, pp. 147–48.

13. H. Melville, *Moby-Dick*, in *Complete Works* 8:9.

14. *Letters of Melville*, p. 79.

15. F. M. Dostoevskij, *Zapiski iz podpol'ja*, in *Polnoe sobranie* 4:194–95.

Chapter 6

1. A. J. Ayer, *The Problem of Knowledge* (Harmondsworth: Penguin, 1956), pp. 184, 186–87.

2. Maurice S. Friedman, *Problematic Rebel: Melville, Dostoievsky, Kafka, Camus*, rev. ed. (Chicago: Univ. of Chicago Press, 1970), pp. 52, 151.

3. Martin Buber, *Pointing the Way*, ed. and trans. Maurice Friedman (New York: Harper & Brothers, 1957), pp. 224, 229.

4. Northrop Frye, *The Great Code: The Bible and Literature* (New York: Harcourt Brace Jovanovich, 1982), pp. 181, passim.

5. Theodore Ziolkowski, *Fictional Transfigurations of Jesus* (Princeton: Princeton Univ. Press, 1972), p. 104.

6. Ibid.

7. Milton Stern, *The Fine Hammered Steel of Herman Melville* (Urbana: Univ. of Illinois Press, 1957), p. 207.

8. Martin Leonard Pops, *The Melville Archetype* (Kent, Ohio: Kent State Univ. Press, 1970), p. 32.

9. Nathalia Wright, *Melville's Use of the Bible* (Durham, N.C.: Duke Univ. Press, 1949), p. 16.

10. D. M. Fiene, "Bartleby the Christ," in *Studies in the Minor and Later Works of Melville*, ed. Raymona E. Hull (Hartford: Transcendental Books, 1970), p. 21.

11. Hans Prager, *Die Weltanschauung Dostojewskis* (Hildesheim: N.p., 1923), p. 203, as quoted in Robert L. Belknap, *The Structure of* The Brothers Karamazov (The Hague and Paris: Mouton, 1967), p. 10.

12. Jakov Golosovker, *Dostoevskij i Kant* (Moscow: AN SSSR, 1963), pp. 139–40.

13. Ibid.

14. *The Letters of Herman Melville*, ed. Merrell R. Davis and William H. Gilman (New Haven: Yale Univ. Press, 1960), p. 127.

15. F. M. Dostoevskij, *Pis'ma,* ed. A. S. Dolinin (Moscow and Leningrad: Gosizdat, 1930), 2:71.

Chapter 7

1. *The Melville Log: A Documentary Life of Herman Melville, 1819–1891,* ed. Jay Leyda, 2 vols. (New York: Harcourt, Brace, 1951), 2:plate IX.
2. *The Letters of Herman Melville,* ed. Merrell R. Davis and William H. Gilman (New Haven: Yale Univ. Press, 1960), p. 235.
3. H. Melville, *Typee,* in *Complete Works,* ed. Raymond Weaver (London: Constable, 1922–24), 1:91.
4. Ibid., p. 89.
5. Ibid., p. 296.
6. Ibid., pp. 7–8.
7. Ibid., p. 8.
8. Martin Leonard Pops, *The Melville Archetype* (Kent, Ohio: Kent State Univ. Press, 1970), p. 27.
9. H. Melville, *Typee,* in *Complete Works* 1:302.
10. Ibid., p. 28.
11. *Letters of Melville,* p. 260.
12. *Melville Log* 2:703–4.
13. *Letters of Melville,* pp. 91–92.
14. Valerian Majkov, *Sočinenija v dvux tomax* (Kiev: Fuks, 1903), 1:27, as quoted in *Dostoevsky and Gogol: Texts and Criticism,* ed. Priscilla Meyer and Stephen Rudy (Ann Arbor: Ardis, 1979), p. xxvi.
15. *Melville Log* 2:648.
16. N. A. Polevoj, *Russkij vestnik,* no. 6 (1842), quoted in *Dostoevsky and Gogol,* p. 165.
17. Jurij Tynjanov, *Dostoevskij i Gogol' (K teorii parodii)* (Petrograd: Opojaz, 1921), p. 6.
18. Ibid., p. 8.
19. Ibid., p. 20.
20. Ibid., p. 21.
21. Ibid., p. 26.
22. F. V. Bulgarin, "Literaturnye tipy," *Severnaja pčela,* no. 22 (1841), quoted in V. V. Vinogradov, *Èvoljucija russkogo naturalizma, Gogol' i Dostoevskij* (Leningrad: Academia, 1929), pp. 303–4.
23. Ivan Panaev, "Rasskazy bez načala i konca," *Literaturnaja gazeta,* no. 1 (1844), quoted in *Èvoljucija russkogo naturalizma,* p. 304.

24. Vinogradov, *Èvoljucija russkogo naturalizma,* p. 312.
25. Ibid., p. 321.
26. *Letters of Melville,* p. 117.
27. S. D. Levickij, *Pravoslavie i narodnost'* (Moscow: Komitet duxovnoj cenzury, 1888), p. 30.
28. Vinogradov, *Èvoljucija russkogo naturalizma,* p. 365.
29. Denham Sutcliffe, *What Shall We Defend?* (Chicago: Univ. of Chicago Press, 1973), pp. 59, 63.
30. Ibid., p. 65.
31. Paul Evdokimov, *Gogol et Dostoïevsky ou la déscente aux Enfers* (Bruges: Desclée de Brouwer, 1961), pp. 275, 281.
32. Joseph Conrad to Cunninghame Graham in French, February 1899, in *Joseph Conrad's Letters to R. B. Cunninghame Graham,* ed. C. T. Watts (London: Cambridge Univ. Press, 1969), p. 117.
33. Dante Alighieri, *The Paradiso of Dante Alighieri,* ed. H. Oelsner, trans. Philip H. Wicksteed (London: J. M. Dent, 1941), p. 307.
34. Ibid., p. 409.
35. *The Unpublished Dostoevsky: Diaries and Notebooks (1860–1881),* ed. Carl R. Proffer, trans. Berczynski, Monter, Boyer, and E. Proffer (Ann Arbor: Ardis, 1973), 1:6.

Chapter 8

1. V. L. Komarovič, "Peterburgskie fel'etony Dostoevskogo," in *Fel'etony sorokovyx godov,* ed. Ju. G. Oksman (Moscow and Leningrad: Academia, 1930), p. 101.
2. Faith Pullin, "Melville's *Typee*: The Failure of Eden," in *New Perspectives on Melville,* ed. Faith Pullin (Edinburgh: Edinburgh Univ. Press, 1978), pp. 7, 6.
3. H. Melville, *The Confidence-Man, His Masquerade,* in *Complete Works,* ed. Raymond Weaver (London: Constable, 1922–24), 12:243–44.
4. Richard Brodhead, "*Mardi*: Creating the Creative," in *New Perspectives on Melville,* pp. 35–36.
5. *The Letters of Herman Melville,* ed. Merrell R. Davis and William H. Gilman (New Haven: Yale Univ. Press, 1960), p. 117.
6. Brodhead, "*Mardi*: Creating the Creative," pp. 41, 48.
7. A. Robert Lee, "*Moby-Dick*: The Tale and the Telling," in *New Perspectives on Melville,* p. 103.
8. *Letters of Melville,* p. 125.

9. Jacques Derrida, *Dissemination*, trans. Barbara Johnson (Chicago: Univ. of Chicago Press, 1981), p. 360.

10. H. Melville, *Mardi*, in *Complete Works* 4:326.

11. Aristotle *Posterior Analytics* 2.1, in *Introduction to Aristotle*, ed. Richard McKeon (New York: Modern Library, 1947).

12. Aristotle *Posterior Analytics* 1.19–22.

13. H. Melville, *Moby-Dick*, in *Complete Works* 7:235–43.

14. H. Melville, *Mardi*, in *Complete Works* 4:328.

15. Ibid., p. 334.

16. Ibid., p. 244.

17. Ibid., p. 161.

18. H. Melville, *White Jacket*, in *Complete Works* 6:1–2.

19. Ibid., p. 5.

20. Ibid., p. 27.

21. Ibid., p. 94.

22. Ibid., p. 215.

23. Ibid., p. 217.

24. Ibid.

25. F. M. Dostoevskij, *Polnoe sobranie xudožestvennyx proizvedenij*, ed. B. Tomaševskij and K. Xalabaev (Moscow and Leningrad: Gosizdat, 1926–30), 5:25.

26. H. Melville, *White Jacket*, in *Complete Works* 6:237.

27. Ibid., p. 98.

28. Leon Howard, *Herman Melville: A Biography* (Berkeley: Univ. of California Press, 1951), p. 137.

29. *The Melville Log: A Documentary Life of Herman Melville, 1819–1891*, ed. Jay Leyda, 2 vols. (New York: Harcourt, Brace, 1951), 1:290.

30. Louis Agassiz and Augustus A. Gould, *Principles in Zoology: Touching the Structure, Development, Distribution, and Natural Arrangement of the Races of Animals, Living and Extinct: with Numerous Illustrations* (Boston: Gould, Kendall & Lincoln, 1848), p. 206.

31. Joseph Flibbert, *Melville and the Art of Burlesque* (Amsterdam: Rodopi, 1974), p. 103.

32. *Letters of Melville*, p. 128.

33. Herman Melville, *Journal up the Straits, October 11, 1856–May 5, 1857*, ed. Raymond Weaver (New York: Colophon, 1935), p. xxii.

34. Ibid., p. 97.

35. Horatio Greenough, "Burke on the Beautiful," in *Form and Func-*

tion: Remarks on Art by Horatio Greenough, ed. H. A. Small (Berkeley: Univ. of California Press, 1947), pp. 89, 95.

36. *Journal up the Straits,* p. iii.

37. Nathaniel Hawthorne, *English Notebooks,* quoted in *Journal up the Straits,* p. xxvi.

38. Jeremiah 18:17, in the New English Bible.

39. H. Melville, *Moby-Dick,* in *Complete Works* 8:187.

Chapter 9

1. F. M. Dostoevskij, *Netočka Nezvanova,* in *Polnoe sobranie xudožestvennyx proizvedenij,* ed. B. Tomaševskij and K. Xalabaev (Moscow and Leningrad: Gosizdat, 1926–30), 2:44–45.

2. F. M. Dostoevskij, "Malen'kij geroj," in *Polnoe sobranie* 2:169.

3. Michael Holquist, *Dostoevsky and the Novel* (Princeton: Princeton Univ. Press, 1977), p. 33.

4. Stewart R. Sutherland, *Atheism and the Rejection of God: Contemporary Philosophy and* The Brothers Karamazov (Oxford: Basil Blackwell, 1977), p. 74.

5. Ibid.

6. M. M. Baxtin, *Problemy poètiki Dostoevskogo* (Moscow: Sovetskij pisatel', 1963), passim.

7. Ludwig Wittgenstein, *The Blue and Brown Books* (New York: Harper & Row, 1965), pp. 41, 5, 167.

8. F. M. Dostoevskij, *Pis'ma,* ed. A. S. Dolinin (Moscow: Goslitizdat, 1959), 4:53.

9. Ibid.

10. Ibid., p. 57.

11. Baxtin, *Problemy poètiki Dostoevskogo,* p. 108.

12. F. M. Dostoevskij, *Unižënnye i oskorblënnye,* in *Polnoe sobranie* 3:48.

13. F. M. Dostoevskij, *Brat'ja Karamazovy,* in *Sobranie sočinenij v desjati tomax,* ed. L. P. Grossman (Moscow: Goslitizdat, 1956–58), 9:406.

14. Ibid., p. 11.

15. Ibid., pp. 11–12.

16. Ibid., p. 370.

17. Ibid., pp. 373–74.

18. Ibid., p. 379.

19. Ibid., pp. 381–83.
20. Ibid., pp. 388–90.
21. Ibid., p. 396.

Chapter 10

1. George Orwell, *Dickens, Dali and Others: Studies in Popular Culture* (New York: Reynal & Hitchcock, 1946), pp. 3, 5, 74.
2. H. Melville, "Field Asters," in *The Collected Poems of Herman Melville*, ed. H. P. Vincent (Chicago: Packard & Co., Hendricks House, 1947), p. 269.
3. F. M. Dostoevskij, "Peterburgskie snovidenija v stixax i proze," in *Polnoe sobranie xudožestvennyx proizvedenij*, ed. B. Tomaševskij and K. Xalabaev (Moscow and Leningrad: Gosizdat, 1926–30), 13:156–57.
4. H. Melville, *Clarel: A Poem and Pilgrimage in the Holy Land*, ed. Walter E. Bezanson (New York: Hendricks House, 1960), p. 43.
5. M. D. Mahoney, *Clarel: An Investigation of Spiritual Crisis* (Washington: Catholic Univ. Press, 1958), p. 16.
6. Vincent Kenny, *Herman Melville's* Clarel: *A Spiritual Autobiography* (Hamden, Conn.: Shoe String Press, 1973), pp. 57–69.
7. Ibid., p. 78.
8. Randall Jarrell, *The Third Book of Criticism* (New York: Farrar, Straus & Giroux, 1965), pp. 149–50.
9. Anonymous review in the *Atlantic Monthly*, February 1867, pp. 252–53.
10. Thomas Hunt Morgan, *The Scientific Basis of Evolution* (1932), chap. 10, as quoted by P. B. Medawar in "Stretch Genes," *The New York Review of Books*, July 16, 1981, p. 45.
11. F. M. Dostoevskij, *Neizdannyj Dostoevskij, Literaturnoe nasledstvo No. 83* (Moscow: Nauka, 1971), pp. 173–75.
12. J. G. Knapp, "Melville's *Clarel*: Dynamic Synthesis," in *Studies in the Minor and Later Works of Melville*, ed. Raymona E. Hull (Hartford: Transcendental Books, 1970), p. 75.
13. F. M. Dostoevskij, *The Notebooks for* The Brothers Karamazov, ed. and trans. Edward Wasiolek (Chicago: Univ. of Chicago Press, 1971), p. 43.
14. F. M. Dostoevskij, *Pis'ma*, ed. A. S. Dolinin (Moscow: Goslitizdat, 1959), 4:59.
15. H. Melville, "The Armies of the Wilderness," in *Battle-Pieces*, ed. Sidney Kaplan (Amherst: Univ. of Massachusetts Press, 1972), p. 94.

16. H. Melville, "The Happy Failure," in *Complete Works*, ed. Raymond Weaver (London: Constable, 1922–24), 13:218–19.

17. H. Melville, "Jimmy Rose" and "Poor Man's Pudding and Rich Man's Crumbs," in *Complete Works* 13:266, 209.

18. Walter Benjamin, "Paris, Capital of the Nineteenth Century," in *Reflections*, ed. Peter Demetz, trans. Edmund Jephcott (New York: Harcourt Brace Jovanovich, 1979), p. 148.

19. Boris Pasternak, "Eleven Letters from Boris Pasternak to George Reavey," *Harvard Library Bulletin* 15, no. 4 (October 1967): 328–29.

20. Evert Duyckinck, review of *Whitejacket* in *The Literary World*, as quoted in *The Recognition of Herman Melville*, ed. Hershel Parker (Ann Arbor: Univ. of Michigan Press, 1967), p. 25.

21. H. Melville, "The Lightning-Rod Man," in *Complete Works* 10:179.

22. Charles Nicol, "The Iconography of Evil and Ideal in 'Benito Cereno,' " in *Studies in the Minor and Later Works of Melville*, p. 30.

Selected Bibliography

Primary Sources

Dostoevskij, Fëdor Mixajlovič. *Neizdannyj Dostoevskij. Literaturnoe nasledstvo No. 83.* Moscow: Nauka, 1971.

———. *The Notebooks for* The Brothers Karamazov. Edited and translated by Edward Wasiolek. Chicago: Univ. of Chicago Press, 1971.

———. *The Notebooks for* Crime and Punishment. Edited and translated by Edward Wasiolek. Chicago: Univ. of Chicago Press, 1967.

———. *The Notebooks for* The Possessed. Edited by Edward Wasiolek. Translated by Victor Terras. Chicago: Univ. of Chicago Press, 1968.

———. *The Notebooks for* A Raw Youth. Edited by Edward Wasiolek. Translated by Victor Terras. Chicago: Univ. of Chicago Press, 1969.

———. *Pis'ma.* Edited by A. S. Dolinin. 4 vols. Moscow and Leningrad: Gosizdat—Academia—Goslitizdat, 1928–59.

———. *Polnoe sobranie xudožestvennyx proizvedenij.* Edited by B. Tomaševskij and K. Xalabaev. 13 vols. Moscow and Leningrad: Gosizdat, 1926–30.

———. *Polnoe sobranie sočinenij v tridcati tomax.* Edited by V. G. Bazanov. Leningrad: AN SSSR / Nauka, 1972–86.

———. *Sobranie sočinenij v desjati tomax.* Edited by L. P. Grossman. Moscow: Goslitizdat, 1956–58.

———. *The Unpublished Dostoevsky: Diaries and Notebooks (1860–1881).* Edited by Carl R. Proffer. Translated by Berczynski, Monter, Boyer, and E. Proffer. 3 vols. Ann Arbor: Ardis, 1973–76.

Melville, Herman. *Clarel: A Poem and Pilgrimage in the Holy Land.* Edited by Walter E. Bezanson. New York: Hendricks House, 1960.

———. *The Collected Poems of Herman Melville.* Edited by H. P. Vincent. Chicago: Packard & Co., Hendricks House, 1947.

———. *The Complete Stories of Herman Melville.* Edited by Jay Leyda. London: Eyre & Spottiswoode, 1951.

———. *Complete Works.* Edited by Raymond Weaver. 16 vols. London: Constable, 1922–24.

———. *Journal of a Visit to London and the Continent 1849–1850.* Edited by E. M. Metcalf. Cambridge: Harvard Univ. Press, 1948.

———. *Journal up the Straits, October 11, 1856–May 5, 1857.* Edited by Raymond Weaver. New York: Colophon, 1935.

———. *The Letters of Herman Melville.* Edited by Merrell R. Davis and William H. Gilman. New Haven: Yale Univ. Press, 1960.

———. *The Writings of Herman Melville.* Edited by Harrison Hayford, Hershel Parker, and G. Thomas Tanselle. Evanston: Northwestern Univ. Press, 1968–.

Secondary Sources

Adams, Robert Martin. *Nil: Episodes in the Literary Conquest of Void During the Nineteenth Century.* New York: Oxford Univ. Press, 1966.

Al'tman, M. S. "Gogolevskie tradicii v tvorčestve Dostoevskogo." *Slavia* 30 (1961): 443–61.

Arvin, Newton, *Herman Melville.* New York: Sloane, 1950.

Auden, W. H. *The Enchafèd Flood.* New York: Random House, 1950.

Baird, James. *Ishmael: A Study of the Symbolic Mode in Primitivism.* Baltimore: Johns Hopkins Univ. Press, 1956.

Baxtin, M. M. *Problemy poètiki Dostoevskogo.* Moscow: Sovetskij pisatel', 1963. (First published as *Problemy tvorčestva Dostoevskogo* [Moscow: Priboj, 1929].)

Bel'čikov, N. F. *Dostoevskij v processe petraševcev.* Moscow: Nauka, 1971.

Belkin, A., et al., eds. *F. M. Dostoevskij v russkoj kritike.* Moscow: Goslitizdat, 1956.

Belknap, Robert L. *The Structure of* The Brothers Karamazov. The Hague and Paris: Mouton, 1967.

Bem, A. L. *Dostoevskij: psixoanalitičeskie ètjudy.* Berlin: Petropolis, 1938.

Bernstein, John. *Pacifism and Rebellion in the Writings of Herman Melville.* The Hague: Mouton, 1964.

Berthoff, Werner. *The Example of Melville.* Princeton: Princeton Univ. Press, 1962.

Bickley, R. Bruce, Jr. *The Method of Melville's Short Fiction.* Durham, N.C.: Duke Univ. Press, 1975.

Blackmur, R. P. *Eleven Essays in the European Novel.* New York: Harcourt, Brace & World, 1964.

———. *The Expense of Greatness.* New York: Arrow, 1940.

Bowen, Merlin. *The Long Encounter: Self and Experience in the Writings of Herman Melville.* Chicago: Univ. of Chicago Press, 1960.

Brodskij, N. L., ed. *Tvorčeskij put' Dostoevskogo: sbornik statej.* Leningrad: Sejatel', 1924.

Brodtkorb, Paul, Jr. *Ishmael's White World: A Phenomenological Reading of* Moby Dick. New Haven: Yale Univ. Press, 1965.

Cambon, Glauco. "La Caccia Ermineutica a *Moby Dick*." *Studi americani* 8 (1962): 9–19.

Cameron, Sharon. *The Corporeal Self: Allegories of the Body in Melville and Hawthorne.* Baltimore: Johns Hopkins Univ. Press, 1981.

Camp, James Edwin. "An Unfulfilled Romance: Image, Symbol and Allegory in Herman Melville's *Clarel*." *Dissertation Abstracts* 27 (1966): 472A.

Canaday, Nicholas, Jr. "A New Reading of 'Benito Cereno.' " In *Studies in American Literature*, edited by Waldo McNeir and Leo B. Levy, pp. 49–57. Baton Rouge: Louisiana State Univ. Press, 1960.

Carr, E. H. *Dostoevsky and Romantic Realism.* Cambridge: Cambridge Univ. Press, 1965.

Chapple, Richard. *A Dostoevsky Dictionary.* Ann Arbor: Ardis, 1983.

Charters, Ann. *Olson/Melville: A Study in Affinity.* San Francisco: Oyez, 1968.

Chase, Richard. *Herman Melville: A Critical Study.* New York: Macmillan, 1949.

———, ed. *Melville: A Collection of Critical Essays.* Englewood Cliffs: Prentice Hall, 1962.

Čirkov, N. M. *O stile Dostoevskogo.* Moscow: AN SSSR, 1963.

Cohen, Hennig. "Wordplay on Personal Names in the Writings of Herman Melville." *Tennessee Studies in Literature* 8 (1963): 85–97.

Connolly, Cyril, ed. *The Modern Movement.* London: André Deutsch, 1965.

Cowan, Bernard. *Exiled Waters:* Moby-Dick *and the Crisis of Allegory.* Baton Rouge: Louisiana State Univ. Press, 1982.

Creeger, George R. "Color Symbolism in the Works of Herman Melville, 1846–1852." *Dissertation Abstracts* 25 (1964): 6620.

Dahlberg, Edward. "*Moby-Dick*—An Hamitic Dream." *Literary Review* 4 (1960): 87–118.

D'Avanzo, Mario L. "Ahab, the Grecian Pantheon and Shelley's *Prometheus Unbound*: The Dynamics of Myth in *Moby-Dick*." *Books at Brown* 24 (1971): 19–44.

Davis, M. R. *Melville's* Mardi: *A Chartless Voyage.* New Haven: Yale Univ. Press, 1952.

Dillingham, William B. *Melville's Later Novels.* Athens: Univ. of Georgia Press, 1986.

———. *Melville's Short Fiction 1853–1856.* Athens: Univ. of Georgia Press, 1977.

Dolinin, A. S. *Dostoevskij. Materialy i issledovanija.* Leningrad: AN SSSR, 1935.

———. *F. M. Dostoevskij: stat'i i materialy.* Vol. 1, Petrograd: Mysl', 1922. Vol. 2, Moscow and Leningrad: Mysl', 1925.

———. *Poslednie romany Dostoevskogo.* Moscow: AN SSSR, 1963.

Drouilly, Jean. *Dostoïevski et l'Europe en 1873.* Ottawa: Editions Leméac, 1969.

Edinger, Edward P. *Melville's* Moby-Dick: *A Jungian Commentary.* New York: New Directions, 1978.

Evdokimov, Paul. *Gogol et Dostoievsky ou la déscente aux Enfers.* Bruges: Desclée de Brouwer, 1961.

Fanger, Donald. *Dostoevsky and Romantic Realism.* Cambridge: Harvard Univ. Press, 1965.

Feidelson, Charles, Jr. Introduction and notes to *Moby-Dick.* Indianapolis: Bobbs-Merrill, 1964.

Finkelstein, Dorothée M. *Melville's Orienda.* New Haven: Yale Univ. Press, 1961.

Fleishman, I. P. "Melville's Use of Language in *Moby Dick.*" Master's thesis, Wesleyan University, 1967.

Flibbert, Joseph. *Melville and the Art of Burlesque.* Amsterdam: Rodopi, 1974.

Frank, Joseph. *Dostoevsky: The Seeds of Revolt, 1821–1849.* Princeton: Princeton Univ. Press, 1976.

———. *Dostoevsky: The Stir of Liberation, 1860–1865.* Princeton: Princeton Univ. Press, 1986.

———. *Dostoevsky: The Years of Ordeal, 1850–1859.* Princeton: Princeton Univ. Press, 1983.

———. "Nihilism and 'Notes from Underground.' " *Slavic Review* 69 (1961): 1–33.

Fridlender, G. M. *Realizm Dostoevskogo.* Leningrad: Nauka, 1964.

Friedman, Maurice S. *Problematic Rebel: Melville, Dostoievsky, Kafka, Camus.* Rev. ed. Chicago: Univ. of Chicago Press, 1970.

Frye, Northrop. *The Great Code: The Bible and Literature.* New York: Harcourt Brace Jovanovich, 1982.

Fülop-Miller, René. *Fyodor Dostoevsky.* Translated by Richard and Clara Winston. New York: Charles Scribner's Sons, 1950.

Gardner, John. "Bartleby: Art and Social Commitment." *Philological*

Quarterly 43 (1964): 87–98.

Gibian, George. "Traditional Symbolism in *Crime and Punishment.*" *PMLA* 70 (December 1955): 979–96.

Gibson, A. Boyce. *The Religion of Dostoevsky.* Philadelphia: Westminster Press, 1973.

Gilmore, Michael T. *Twentieth Century Interpretations of* Moby-Dick. Englewood Cliffs: Prentice Hall, 1977.

Girard, René. *Dostoievski: Du Double à l'unité.* Paris: Grasset, 1964.

Golosovker, Jakov E. *Dostoevskij i Kant.* Moscow: AN SSSR, 1963.

Griffith, Frank C. *Melville and the Quest for God.* Iowa City: Univ. of Iowa Press, 1953.

Grossman, L. P. *Balzac and Dostoevsky.* Translated by L. Karpov. Ann Arbor: Ardis, 1973.

———. *Dostoevskij.* Moscow: Molodaja gvardija, 1965.

———. *Poètika Dostoevskogo.* Moscow: Akademija xudozestvennyx nauk, 1925.

———. *Seminarii po Dostoevskomu.* Moscow and Petrograd: Academia, 1922.

———, ed. *Tvorčestvo Dostoevskogo 1821–1881–1921 gg. Sbornik statej i materialov.* Odessa: Vseukrajnskoe gosizdat, 1921.

Guardini, Romano. *Religiöse Gestalten in Dostoiewskijs Werk.* (Rev. ed. of *Der Mensch und sein Glaube.*) Munich: Kösel, 1964.

Gus', M. *Idei i obrazy F. M. Dostoevskogo.* Moscow: Goslitizdat, 1971.

Hauck, R. B. *A Cheerful Nihilism: Confidence and "The Absurd" in American Humorous Fiction.* Bloomington: Indiana Univ. Press, 1971.

Herbert, Thomas W. Moby Dick *and Calvinism, A World Dismantled.* New Brunswick: Rutgers Univ. Press, 1977.

Hillway, Tyrus. *Melville and 19th Century Science.* New Haven: Yale Univ. Press, 1944.

Holquist, Michael. *Dostoevsky and the Novel.* Princeton: Princeton Univ. Press, 1977.

Howard, Leon. *Herman Melville: A Biography.* Berkeley: Univ. of California Press, 1951.

Hull, Raymona E., ed. *Studies in the Minor and Later Works of Melville.* Hartford: Transcendental Books, 1970. This book includes:

B. C. Bach, "Narrative Technique and Structure in *Pierre*"

R. B. Browne, "Two Views of Commitment: 'The Paradise of Bachelors' and 'The Tartarus of Maids' "

M. A. Campbell, "A Quiet Crusade: Melville's Tales of the Fifties"

Marjorie Dew, "The Prudent Captain Vere"

D. M. Fiene, "Bartleby the Christ"
J. L. George, "Israel Potter: The Height of Patriotism"
V. S. Kenny, "Clarel's Rejection of the Titans"
J. G. Knapp, "Melville's *Clarel*: Dynamic Synthesis"
Paul McCarthy, "Affirmative Elements in *The Confidence Man*"
M. E. Mengeling, "Through the 'Encantadas': An Experienced Guide and You"
Winifred Neff, "Satirical Use of a 'Silly Reference' in *Israel Potter*"
Charles Nicol, "The Iconography of Evil and Ideal in 'Benito Cereno' "
Hershel Parker, "Melville's Satire of Emerson and Thoreau: An Evaluation of Evidence"
R. E. Ray, "Benito Cereno: Babo as Leader"
E. H. Rosenberry, "Melville and His *Mosses*"
John Seelye, "The Contemporary 'Bartleby' "
D. R. Swanson, "The Exercise of Irony in 'Benito Cereno' "
Maurita Willett, "The Silences of Herman Melville"

Ivanov, Vjačeslav. *Freedom and the Tragic Life.* London: Harvill Press, 1952.

Ivask, George. "Dostoevsky's Wit." *The Russian Review* 21 (1962): 154–64.

Jackson, Robert L. *Dostoevsky's Quest for Form: A Study of His Philosophy of Art.* New Haven: Yale Univ. Press, 1966.

———, ed. *Twentieth-Century Interpretations of* Crime and Punishment. Englewood Cliffs: Prentice Hall, 1974.

Jaffé, David. *The Stormy Petrel and the Whale: Some Origins of* Moby-Dick. Baltimore: Port City Press, 1976.

Jones, Malcolm V. *Dostoevsky: The Novel of Discord.* London: Elek Books, 1976.

Jones, Peter. *Philosophy and the Novel.* Oxford: Clarendon Press, 1975.

Kabat, Geoffrey. *Ideology and Imagination: The Image of Society in Dostoevsky.* New York: Columbia Univ. Press, 1978.

Kenny, Vincent. *Herman Melville's* Clarel: *A Spiritual Autobiography.* Hamden, Conn.: Shoe String Press, 1973.

Keyssar, Alexander. *Melville's* Israel Potter: *Reflections on the American Dream.* Cambridge: Harvard Univ. Press, 1969.

Komarovič, V. L. "Peterburgskie fel'etony Dostoevskogo." In *Fel'etony sorokovyx godov,* edited by Ju. G. Oksman, pp. 89–126. Moscow and Leningrad: Academia, 1930.

Kovalëv, Ju. V. *German Melvill i amerikanskij romantizm.* Leningrad: Goslitizdat, 1972.

Kramer, Aaron. *Melville's Poetry: Toward the Enlarged Heart.* Rutherford: Fairleigh Dickinson Univ. Press, 1972.

Kuhlman, Susan. *Knave, Fool and Genius: The Confidence Man as He Appears in Nineteenth Century American Fiction.* Chapel Hill: Univ. of North Carolina Press, 1973.

Levin, Harry. *The Power of Blackness: Hawthorne, Poe, Melville.* New York: Knopf, 1958.

Levickij, S. D. *Pravoslavie i narodnost'.* Moscow: Komitet duxovnoj cenzury, 1888.

Lewis, R. W. B. *The American Adam: Innocence, Tragedy and Tradition in the Nineteenth Century.* Chicago: Univ. of Chicago Press, 1955.

Leyda, Jay, ed. *The Melville Log: A Documentary Life of Herman Melville, 1819–1891.* 2 vols. New York: Harcourt, Brace, 1951.

Lord, R., ed. *Dostoevsky: Essays and Perspectives.* Berkeley: Univ. of California Press, 1970.

Losskij, N. *Dostoevskij i ego xristianskoe miroponimanie.* New York: Chekhov Pub., 1953.

Lucid, Robert R. "The Influence of *Two Years Before the Mast* on Herman Melville." *American Literature* 31, no. 3 (1959): 243–56.

Mahoney, M. D. Clarel: *An Investigation of Spiritual Crisis.* Washington: Catholic Univ. Press, 1958.

Mann, Jurij. "Filosofija i poètika 'Natural'noj školy.' " In *Problemy tipologii russkogo realizma,* edited by N. L. Stepanov and Ju. R. Foxt. Moscow: AN SSSR, 1969.

Marcus, Mordecai. "Melville's Bartleby as a Psychological Double." *College English* 23 (1962): 365–68.

Matlaw, Ralph E. The Brothers Karamazov: *Novelistic Technique.* The Hague: Mouton, 1957.

———. "Thanatos and Eros." *Slavic and East European Journal* 4 (1960): 222–42.

Matthiessen, F. O. "Melville." In his *American Renaissance,* pp. 371–514. London and New York: Oxford Univ. Press, 1941.

Mayoux, Jean Jacques. *Melville.* Translated by J. Ashbery. New York: Grove, 1960.

Metcalf, Eleanor Melville. *Herman Melville, Cycle and Epicycle.* Cambridge: Harvard Univ. Press, 1953.

Meyer, Priscilla, and Stephen Rudy, eds. *Dostoevsky and Gogol: Texts and Criticism.* Ann Arbor: Ardis, 1979.

Miller, Edwin H. *Melville.* New York: George Braziller, 1975.

Miller, James E., Jr. *A Reader's Guide to Herman Melville.* New York: Farrar, Straus & Cudahy, 1962.

Močul'skij, Konstantin. *Dostoevskij: Žizn' i tvorčestvo.* Paris: YMCA Press, 1947.

Modern Fiction Studies 4, no. 3 (1958). Special Dostoevsky number including:

Victor E. Amend, "Theme and Form in *The Brothers Karamazov*"

Louise Dauner, "Raskolnikov in Search of a Soul"

George Gibian, "The Grotesque in Dostoevsky"

Simon O. Lesser, "Saint and Sinner—Dostoevsky's *Idiot*"

Carl Niemeyer, "Raskolnikov and Lafcadio"

Nathan Rosen, "Breaking Out of the Underground: The 'Failure' of *A Raw Youth*"

Modern Fiction Studies 8, no. 3 (1962). Special Melville number including:

Sister Mary Ellen, "Duplicate Imagery in *Moby-Dick*"

John T. Frederick, "Symbol and Theme in Melville's *Israel Potter*"

Jesse D. Green, "Diabolism, Pessimism and Democracy: Notes on Melville and Conrad"

Allen Hayman, "The Real and the Original: Herman Melville's Theory of Prose Fiction"

Howard C. Horsford, "The Design of the Argument in *Moby-Dick*"

William T. Stafford, "The New *Billy Budd* and the Novelistic Fallacy"

Kingsley Widmer, "The Negative Affirmation: Melville's 'Bartleby' "

Moore, Maxine. *That Lonely Game: Melville,* Mardi *and the Almanac.* Columbia: Univ. of Missouri Press, 1975.

Morson, Gary. *The Boundaries of Genre: Dostoevsky's* Diary of a Writer *and the Traditions of Literary Utopia.* Austin: Univ. of Texas Press, 1981.

Mossman, Elliott D. "Dostoevskij's Early Works: The More than Rational Distortion." *Slavic and East European Journal* 10 (1966): 268–78.

Mumford, Lewis. *Herman Melville.* New York: Harcourt, Brace, 1929.

Nnolim, Charles E. *Melville's "Benito Cereno": A Study in Meaning of Name Symbolism.* New York: New Voices, 1974.

Oksman, Ju. G., ed. *Fel'etony sorokovyx godov.* Moscow and Leningrad: Academia, 1930.

Olson, Charles. *Call Me Ishmael.* New York: Reynal & Hitchcock, 1947.

———. "The Growth of Herman Melville, Prose Writer and Poetic Thinker." Master's thesis, Wesleyan University, 1933.

———. *Letter for Melville*. Black Mountain: Black Mountain Workshop, 1951.

Parker, Hershel, ed. *The Recognition of Herman Melville: Selected Criticism Since 1846*. Ann Arbor: Univ. of Michigan Press, 1967.

———, and Harrison Hayford, eds. Moby-Dick *as Doubloon*. New York: W. W. Norton, 1970.

Passage, Charles. *Dostoevsky the Adapter: A Study in Dostoevsky's Use of the Tales of Hoffmann*. Chapel Hill: Univ. of North Carolina Press, 1954.

Percival, Milton O. *A Reading of* Moby-Dick. New York: Octagon, 1967.

Pereverzev, V. F. F. M. *Dostoevskij*. Moscow and Leningrad: Gosizdat, 1925.

Pops, Martin Leonard. *The Melville Archetype*. Kent, Ohio: Kent State Univ. Press, 1970.

Pullin, Faith, ed. *New Perspectives on Melville*. Edinburgh: Edinburgh Univ. Press, 1978. This book includes:

- Richard H. Brodhead, "*Mardi*: Creating the Creative"
- Arnold Goldman, "Melville's England"
- Harrison Hayford, "Unnecessary Duplicates: A Key to the Writing of *Moby-Dick*"
- Brian Higgins and Hershel Parker, "The Flawed Grandeur of Melville's *Pierre*"
- Eric Homberger, "Melville, Lt. Guert Gansevoort and Authority: An Essay in Biography"
- Q. D. Leavis, "Melville: The 1853–6 Phase"
- A. Robert Lee, "*Moby-Dick*: The Tale and the Telling"
- C. N. Marlove, "An Organic Hesitancy: Theme and Style in *Billy Budd*"
- Eric Mottram, "Orpheus and Measured Forms: Law, Madness and Reticence in Melville"
- Faith Pullin, "Melville's *Typee*: The Failure of Eden"
- Larzer Ziff, "Shakespeare and Melville's America"

Rampersad, Arnold. *Melville's* Israel Potter: *A Pilgrimage and Progress*. Bowling Green: Bowling Green Univ. Popular Press, 1969.

Rehm, Walter. "Experimentum suae medietatis. Eine Studie zur dichterischen Gestaltung des Unglaubens bei Jean Paul und Dostojewski." In *Jahrbuch des Freien Deutshcen Hochstifts Frankfurt-am-Main*. Halle: Niemener, 1940.

Roe, Ivan. *The Breath of Corruption: An Interpretation of Dostoevsky.* London: Hutchinson, 1946.

Rosenberry, Edward H. *Melville.* London: Routledge & Kegan Paul, 1979.

———. *Melville and the Comic Spirit.* Cambridge: Harvard Univ. Press, 1955.

Roundtree, Thomas J. *Critics on Melville.* Coral Gables: Univ. of Miami Press, 1972.

Rozanov, V. V. *Legenda o velikom inkvizitore F. M. Dostoevskogo.* St. Petersburg: M. V. Pirožkov, 1906.

Rževskij, L. *Tri temy po Dostoevskomu.* Frankfurt-am-Main: Posev, 1972.

Sachs, Viola. *La contre-Bible de Melville:* Moby-Dick *déchiffré.* The Hague and Paris: Mouton, 1975.

Schless, Howard H. "Flaxman, Dante and Melville's *Pierre.*" *Bulletin of the New York Public Library* 64 (1960): 65–82.

Sedgwick, William E. *Herman Melville: The Tragedy of Mind.* Cambridge: Harvard Univ. Press, 1944.

Seduro, Vladimir. *Dostoyevski in Russian Literary Criticism 1846–1956.* New York: Columbia Univ. Press, 1957.

Seelye, John. *Melville.* Evanston: Northwestern Univ. Press, 1970.

Shattuck, Roger. "Two Inside Narratives: *Billy Budd* and *l'Étranger.*" *Texas Studies in Literature and Language* 4 (1962): 314–20.

Šklovskij, V. *Za i protiv. Zametki o Dostoevskom.* Moscow: Sovetskij pisatel', 1967.

Shulman, Robert. "The Serious Function of Melville's Phallic Jokes." *American Literature* 33 (May 1961): 179–94.

Simmons, Ernest J. *Dostoevsky: The Making of a Novelist.* London and New York: Oxford Univ. Press, 1940.

———. *Introduction to Russian Realism.* Bloomington: Indiana Univ. Press, 1965.

Simon, Jean. *Herman Melville, Marin, Métaphysicien et Poète.* Paris: Boivin, 1939.

Solomon, P. C. *Dickens and Melville.* New York: Columbia Univ. Press, 1975.

Springer, Norman. "Bartleby and the Terror of Limitation." *PMLA* 80 (1965): 410–18.

Stepanov, N. L., et al., eds. *Tvorčestvo F. M. Dostoevskogo.* Moscow: AN SSSR, 1959. This book includes:

G. L. Abramovič, "K voprosu o prirode i xaraktere realizma Dostoevskogo"

A. A. Belkin, "*Brat'ja Karamazovy* (Social'no-filosofskaja problematika)" and "O realizme Dostoevskogo"
B. A. Bjalik, "Dostoevskij i dostoevščina v ocenkax Gor'kogo"
A. V. Čičerin, "Poètičeskij stroj jazyka v romanax Dostoevskogo"
G. M. Fridlender, "Roman *Idiot*"
L. P. Grossman, "Dostoevskij-xudožnik"
D. O. Zaslavskij, "Zametki o jumore i satire v proizvedenijax Dostoevskogo"
and others

Stern, Milton R. *The Fine Hammered Steel of Herman Melville.* Urbana: Univ. of Illinois Press, 1957.

———, ed. *Discussions of* Moby Dick. Boston: D. C. Heath, 1960.

Stuart, Frank M. *Herman Melville's Picture Gallery: Sources and Types of the "Pictorial" Chapters of* Moby-Dick. Fairhaven: E. J. Lefkowicz, 1986.

Sutcliffe, Denham. *What Shall We Defend?* Chicago: Univ. of Chicago Press, 1973.

Sutherland, Stewart R. *Atheism and the Rejection of God: Contemporary Philosophy and* The Brothers Karamazov. Oxford: Basil Blackwell, 1977.

Sweeney, Gerald M. *Melville's Use of Classical Mythology.* Amsterdam: Rodopi, 1975.

Terras, Victor. "Problems of Human Existence in the Works of the Young Dostoevsky." *The Slavic Review* 23 (1964): 79–91.

Thompson, Lawrance. *Melville's Quarrel with God.* Princeton: Princeton Univ. Press, 1952.

———. "*Moby-Dick*: One Way to Cut In." *Carrell* 3, no. 3 (1962): 1–12.

Tomaševskij, B. V. *Teorija literatury: Poètika.* 4th ed. Moscow: Gosizdat, 1928.

Trubetskoj, N. S. *Dostoevskij als Künstler.* The Hague: Mouton, 1964.

Cejtlin, A. G. *Povest' o bednom činovnike Dostoevskogo (K istorii odnogo sjužeta).* Moscow: Gosizdat, 1923.

Vetlovskaja, V. E. *Poètika romana* Brat'ja Karamazovy. Leningrad: Nauka, 1977.

Vincent, Howard P. *The Tailoring of Melville's* White-jacket. Evanston: Northwestern Univ. Press, 1970.

———. *The Trying-Out of* Moby Dick. Carbondale: Southern Illinois Univ. Press, 1965.

———, ed. *Melville Annual 1965, a Symposium: Bartleby, the Scrivener.* Kent, Ohio: Kent State Univ. Press, 1966.

———, ed. *Twentieth Century Interpretations of* Billy Budd. Englewood Cliffs: Prentice Hall, 1971.

Vinogradov, V. V. *Èvoljucija russkogo naturalizma: Gogol' i Dostoevskij.* Leningrad: Academia, 1929.

———. *O jazyke xudožestvennoj literatury.* Moscow: Goslitizdat, 1959.

Wadlington, Warwick. *The Confidence Game in American Literature.* Princeton: Princeton Univ. Press, 1975.

Warren, R. P. "Melville the Poet." *The Kenyon Review* 8, no. 2 (Spring 1946): 208–23.

Wasiolek, Edward. "*Aut Caesar, aut nihil:* A Study of Dostoevsky's Moral Dialectic." *PMLA* 78 (1963): 89–97.

———. *Dostoevsky: The Major Fiction.* Cambridge: M.I.T. Press, 1964.

Weaver, Raymond. *Herman Melville, Mariner and Mystic.* New York: George H. Doran, 1921.

Wellek, René, ed. *Dostoevsky: A Collection of Critical Essays.* Englewood Cliffs: Prentice Hall, 1962.

Winner, T. G. "Dostoevsky and Romantic Aesthetics." *Yearbook of Comparative and General Literature* 9 (1962): 36–39.

Wright, Nathalia. *Melville's Use of the Bible.* Durham, N.C.: Duke Univ. Press, 1949.

Yarmolinsky, Avrahm. *Dostoevsky, His Life and Art.* Rev. ed. New York: Grove, 1960.

Zander, L. A. *Dostoevsky.* Translated by Natalie Duddington. London: SCM Press, 1948.

Ziolkowski, Theodore. *Fictional Transfigurations of Jesus.* Princeton: Princeton Univ. Press, 1972.

Zoellner, Robert. *The Salt-sea Mastodon.* Berkeley: Univ. of California Press, 1973.

Index